Bruce Bugbee is brilliant! I always enjoy lea
speaks to our core leadership. I enthusiastic:
purpose-driven church that wants to mobilize 1

Rick Warren, pastor, Saddleback Community Church

Bruce Bugbee has been a pioneer and leader in helping ordinary followers of
Jesus live an extraordinary life of meaning and fruitfulness. I have become a
better leader and more faithful disciple because of the ideas in this book.

Kevin G. Harney, lead pastor of Shoreline Church
and cofounder of Organic Outreach International

All of us who have been doing this work over the last couple of decades are
aware that we are building on the work of Bruce Bugbee. *What You Do Best* is
his most important work yet.

Rob Wegner, founding leader, Kansas City Underground,
and coauthor of *The Starfish and the Spirit*

I don't know of another person who has devoted more prayer, study, thought,
time, and energy to helping people find their ministry roles than Bruce
Bugbee. I strongly encourage you to let him ignite your passion as you read
What You Do Best.

Don Cousins, lead pastor, Discovery Church, Orlando, Florida

Bruce Bugbee has faithfully responded to God's call on his life by teaching
gift-based ministry and serving God's people through outstanding, user-
friendly tools accessible to all who desire to teach and learn from them.

Sue Mallory, author of *The Equipping Church*

This book can change your life and your ministry. It's a must-read for anyone
who desires to successfully lead and serve!

Dr. Colette Cozean, president, East Africa Partnership

The principles of *What You Do Best* have made a significant difference in my
marketplace leadership and consulting. I've been able to influence thousands
with the teachings from this book.

Ken Bado, CEO, GMB Consulting, LLC

Spiritual gifts are supernatural abilities. *What You Do Best* accelerates this core truth and links it to our relational style and life passion.

Charles Halley, author of *The House of Jesus*

I can't think of a more important investment of a person's time than understanding who God created them to be and what he calls them to do. *What You Do Best* shines a bright light on one's journey of self-understanding.

Tom Cramer, executive for vision and mission,
Presbytery of Los Ranchos, California

If you're looking to help others discover how they can make an impact in the world, I would start here.

Shawn Andrews, lead equipping pastor, Daybreak Church,
Mechanicsburg, Pennsylvania

Rejecting both cookie-cutter models and hyper-individualized systems, Bruce Bugbee walks leaders through the whys and hows of gift-based ministry and demonstrates that the Spirit builds wholes that are greater than the sums of their parts.

Tim Breen, lead pastor, First Reformed Church, Orange City, Iowa

A handbook that aptly summarizes biblical principles into a potent guide for everyday Christian living. This is a book worth reading and rereading for insight and practical application!

Samuel Wainaina Gichuhi, projects coordinator,
Africa Inland Church (AIC), Kenya

So many today suffer from role confusion. They are willing to serve, but they haven't been able to align their passions with their spiritual gifts. This book has helped many people understand what they can do best—and how.

Josphat Kairu, director of communications,
East Africa Partnership, Kenya

I recommend Bruce Bugbee's wisdom and insights to anyone who is seeking to find their right place of service within the kingdom of God.

Eric Carpenter, lead pastor, Springs Community Church,
Colorado Springs, Colorado

What you read in this book, Bruce Bugbee taught me as a young Christian many years ago. If you desire an impactful ministry, I urge you to read this book.

Bob Bouwer, senior pastor, Faith Church,
South Chicagoland and Northwest Indiana

Filled with keen insights and practical tools, *What You Do Best* helps us rediscover our God-given shape, leading to a more satisfying life and greater kingdom impact.

Dr. Bill Hoyt, president, NexStep Coaching and Consulting,
Laguna Woods, California

Understanding who we are is crucial because ministry flows out of our being. Bruce Bugbee helps us find an answer to the question, "Am I the right person, in the right place, for a right reason, at the right time?"

Igors Rautmanis, secretary of staff and team development,
International Fellowship of Evangelical Students, Latvia

What You Do Best has changed the way I lead and speak because I now understand the way I'm wired to do so! If you're looking to put your passions into practice and experience a vibrant life, this book is a powerful tool.

Ali Gentry, CEO and founder of Vibrant Ministries & ARISE

Are you seeking direction and alignment, or simply trying to avoid burnout? Whatever the case, this book is a must-read and a staple in your library.

Lisa J. Haase, founder and chief strategist,
Rise Consulting International, LLC

Bruce Bugbee's work on spiritual gifts has been foundational to my own spiritual journey and ministry with Christian college students.

Dr. Edee Schulze, vice president for student life,
Westmont College, Santa Barbara, California

What You Do Best is a fantastic read that helps you recognize your spiritual gifts and how important they are in our world. Bruce's writing is encouraging and comes to life as you read.

Jenae Slater, teacher and leader of WyldLife,
Goodland Church, Santa Barbara, California

I love the emphasis Bruce Bugbee places on people development instead of program development. When it comes to people development, you start with the wisdom of the crown of God's creation and let people reflect the creativity of their Creator in the world.

Tim Vink, director of spiritual leadership and outreach, Alliance of Reformed Churches

What You Do Best has helped me embrace myself for who I am. This means continuing in my current work while also serving in the church as a pastor. I do not need to suppress one over the other.

Samer Najm, Baker Hughes/a GE Company, Dubai, United Arab Emirates

This is a timely word for a culture that needs to hear they have a part to play in the mission of God, a message every believer needs to hear!

Chestly Lunday, founder, KingCity and Aneeko, Glendale, Arizona

Any organization interested in improving its leadership or management team can find many consultants and much literature in the marketplace. Bruce Bugbee offers a unique approach.

Willy Tjen, elder, New Life Community Church, Artesia, California

What You Do Best should be in the personal library of every student, minister, and Christian in the marketplace. It's for anyone who is thirsty for a solid, biblically understandable foundation for their personal growth and life purpose.

Dr. Andrés Serrano, senior pastor, La Senda Reformed Church, and president, Radio Impacto Network, USA/Dominican Republic

Today we have teachers who stray from biblical truths and practices into humanistic philosophies that resemble the truth but actually promote false teachings. Bruce Bugbee keeps us focused on doing God's will his way.

Dr. Brígido Cabrera, associate academic dean, Mints Seminary, Miami, Florida, and coordinator for the Dominican Republic

WHAT YOU DO BEST

Unleashing the Power of
Your Spiritual Gifts, Relational Style,
and Life Passion

Includes assessments to create your customized
RIGHT4 YOU Profile™

BRUCE BUGBEE

ZONDERVAN
REFLECTIVE

ZONDERVAN REFLECTIVE

What You Do Best
Copyright © 1995, 2005, 2022 by Bruce Bugbee

Requests for information should be addressed to:
Zondervan, *3900 Sparks Dr. SE, Grand Rapids, Michigan 49546*

Zondervan titles may be purchased in bulk for educational, business, fundraising, or sales promotional use. For information, please email SpecialMarkets@Zondervan.com.

ISBN 978-0-310-13940-9 (softcover)

ISBN 978-0-310-13942-3 (audio)

ISBN 978-0-310-13941-6 (ebook)

All Scripture quotations, unless otherwise indicated, are taken from the New American Standard Bible® (NASB), Copyright © 1960, 1971, 1977, 1995, 2020 by The Lockman Foundation. All rights reserved.

Scripture quotations marked NIV are taken from The Holy Bible, New International Version®, NIV®. Copyright © 1973, 1978, 1984, 2011 by Biblica, Inc.® Used by permission of Zondervan. All rights reserved worldwide. www.Zondervan.com. The "NIV" and "New International Version" are trademarks registered in the United States Patent and Trademark Office by Biblica, Inc.®

Scripture quotations marked NLT are taken from the Holy Bible, New Living Translation. © 1996, 2004, 2015 by Tyndale House Foundation. Used by permission of Tyndale House Publishers, Inc., Carol Stream, Illinois 60188. All rights reserved.

Any internet addresses (websites, blogs, etc.) and telephone numbers in this book are offered as a resource. They are not intended in any way to be or imply an endorsement by Zondervan, nor does Zondervan vouch for the content of these sites and numbers for the life of this book.

This book contains stories from the author's career as an executive coach, leadership developer, and pastor. Names have been changed to protect the privacy of individuals listed. Any similarity in detail is purely coincidental.

Cover design: LUCAS Art & Design
Cover art: Creative Market
Interior design: Kait Lamphere

Printed in the United States of America

22 23 24 25 26 27 28 29 30 31 32 /TRM/ 15 14 13 12 11 10 9 8 7 6 5 4 3 2 1

To this generation
of Christ followers

CONTENTS

SECTION 4: The Purposeful You

MY RIGHT4 YOU PROFILE

A NOTE FROM THE AUTHOR

You are the subject of this book. *What You Do Best* equips you to identify and express your unique contribution to this world as an integral part of your relationships, life, and ministry. My desire in writing this book is to help you gain a better understanding of who God made you to be. The biblical principles in these pages can free you to pursue your life's calling with enthusiasm and confidence.

God's Spirit moves across geographical and international boundaries; denominational and theological differences; generational perspectives; and gender, racial, ethnic, and cultural uniqueness—all to bring hope, justice, and healing to our world. Remarkably, he uses you and me to accomplish this. It's our greatest privilege.

In the coming chapters, you'll have the opportunity to examine yourself, assess your relationship with God, and reflect on what you need in order to thrive as the person you were created to be. I encourage you to connect with a few close friends to share your learnings, get their input, and pray for God's insights. I'm confident you'll emerge from the process with a greater understanding of God, his purposes, your calling, and your role in this world.

Anytime we begin to explore our inner selves, it's natural to resist the process. Even if we're not happy or satisfied with certain aspects of our lives, we know that change means leaving behind the comfort of life as we know it, but change is necessary in order to step into all that God made us to be.

PULLING UP STAKES

Many years ago, my friend Bobb shared a story that illustrates this dilemma.

Bobb once spent a day volunteering at an old-time three-ring circus. During a break, he went over to pat an elephant and her baby, who were both shackled to stakes in the ground. He couldn't help but notice that the small stake securing the baby was the same thickness as the one securing her gigantic mother. Given the adult elephant's tremendous strength and size, he thought, *Surely she could break free if she chose.*

The elephant's handler was a man who trained animals for Hollywood movies. When he stopped by to check on the elephants, Bobb asked him, "How is it that you can keep a ten-ton elephant in place with the same size stake you use for this little fellow?" (The "little fellow" weighed only about three hundred pounds.)

"Elephants have great memories," the trainer said. "We begin staking them when they're babies. Day after day, they try to tug away from the stake—maybe ten thousand times over those first months. Eventually they realize they can't possibly get away and they stop trying. At that point, their amazing elephant memory takes over. For the rest of their lives—long after they could easily yank that stake from the ground—they remember it does no good to tug at the stake. They believe they can't get away, and therefore they can't."

Sadly, in some ways, we are like those elephants. When young, we may have heard we aren't very smart, we're clumsy, we're slow, or we don't have any common sense. In our teens, we may have heard we're not very good leaders, we lack initiative, we'll never amount to anything, or we will never be good enough. Those words drive a mental stake into the ground.

For me, one such statement was, "You're not a writer." A mental stake was driven in, and for decades I didn't even try to write anything beyond an email. But I couldn't shake the sense that God had something for me to say, and he wanted me to write about it.

Eventually, I pulled that mental stake out of the ground and began writing. To date, millions of people in fifteen languages around the world have found greater freedom and purpose for their lives through the biblical principles found in this book.

Turns out, I'm a writer after all!

Often, even as adults we can be held back by inaccurate stakes driven into our minds when we were younger. Those stakes limit our freedom, warp our perception of self, and stifle our understanding of who we are created to be.

> *Millions of people in fifteen languages around the world have found greater freedom and purpose for their lives through the biblical principles found in this book.*

Jesus calls us to be what he sees in us, what he created us to be. He invites us to break free from outdated stakes. In Christ, we are no longer bound by the limits that others place in our lives. "If the Son sets you free," he declares, "you really will be free."[1]

Wherever we go and whatever we do, we are free to fulfill the God-given purpose he has created and called us to fulfill, whether through the church, nonprofit work, or marketplace jobs.

"It was for freedom that Christ set us free."[2] Jesus did not die on the cross to make us good; he died to make us free. If we're merely attempting to do the right thing on our own strength, we'll lack joy and power. But those who are truly free experience the fullness and goodness of God.

Mother Teresa once said, "I always say I am a little pencil in God's hand."[3] I trust you will see God's fingerprints in your life as you journey through this book—and as a result you'll become better equipped to live a life that is faithful, fruitful, and fulfilled.

Onward!

Bruce Bugbee

THE CREATED YOU

1 INTENTIONAL CREATION

God created us with intention. He created us by design. He calls us toward the purposes for which he created us and then equips us to succeed in those purposes. He values us deeply and gives us everything we need to make meaningful contributions with our lives.

This biblical concept is easy to understand but a little difficult to implement. How can we be the right people in the right places for the right reasons at the right times? *What You Do Best* equips you to identify and develop your truest self—and unleash your God-given gifts, style, and passions on the world.

How can we be the right people in the right places for the right reasons at the right times?

You are unique by design. Your true self aligns with how God created and called you. He instilled in you a unique set of gifts as a follower of Christ (your spiritual gifts). He wired you with certain preferred ways of doing things (your relational style), and he fired you up with interests and causes that are uniquely you (your life passion).

No one else has your unique blending of spiritual gifts, relational style, and passions. When using your spiritual gifts as God intended, you'll be more competent in your roles. When operating in ways that are consistent with your relational style, you'll function with greater confidence, freedom, and joy. When you're making a difference in one of your areas of passion, you'll be more energized and fulfilled. Life will have more meaning. You'll experience a peace found only in living as your truest self, the person God created you to be.

Your Self

Throughout this book, you'll notice I make a distinction between the words *yourself* and *your self*. This isn't a typo—I do this by design. Self refers to our personhood, our individuality, our holistic identity (physically, emotionally, relationally, and spiritually). Thus "your self" is the interaction and collaboration of your mind, body, and spirit. It's the alignment of your inner and outer selves with integrity and congruity.

When you see "your self," remember you're seeking to explore your whole self—body, mind, and spirit.

So why do so few of us experience this type of living? By way of analogy, let me share a story from my own life.

One of my lifelong dreams was to design and build my own home. Shortly after my family moved to Iowa, I got that opportunity. I sketched some floor plans, and we finalized a design, agreed on costs, purchased a lot, and built the house. It was a lot of work, and when we moved in, I crossed this dream off my bucket list with a great sense of satisfaction.

But as anyone who has built a house can attest, construction costs often exceed expectations, and by the time we moved in, we had no budget left over for landscaping. *I'll just do the landscaping myself,* I thought. *I know how to work a shovel. How hard can it be?*

With a healthy dose of overconfidence, I headed to a local nursery and bought trees, shrubs, flowers, and sod. Over several long weekends, I planted them all and then patted myself on the back for how much money I'd saved. The yard looked great—for a while.

A couple months later, I noticed the plants on one side of the house had died. *I must have bought bad plants,* I thought, and promptly headed back to the nursery. After complaining a bit about the bad plants, I bought replacements, pulled out the dead plants, and installed the lush new ones. Within a few months, they, too, began to fade. What was the problem?

One evening, I was in my backyard watering my near-dead plants in hopes of saving them when my neighbor Tom stopped by. He's an avid gardener, and his yard showed it. He asked what I was doing.

"Trying to save these dying plants," I said. "It's maddening. The first ones I planted died, so I replaced them. Now these are dying too. The nursery keeps selling me sick plants."

"It's not the plants," he said. "It's this location."

Tom then explained that this type of plant needs direct sunlight, but I'd planted them on the north side of the house, where they were in the shade all day long.

I dug up the struggling plants and moved them to a sunny spot on the south side of my yard. They perked right up. I then bought some shade-loving plants for the north side of the house, and each type of plant thrived in its intended environment.

So simple! There was nothing wrong with the plants. The problem was where I put them. Because I didn't know what each plant needed, I planted them in the wrong place. But once in the right environment, they flourished. Imagine that!

> *Because I didn't know what each plant needed, I planted them in the wrong place. But once in the right environment, they flourished.*

Have you heard the expression, "Bloom where you are planted"? Sounds hopeful, right? No one would argue that we should do our best in whatever situation we find ourselves.[1] But what if instead of struggling to bloom where we are planted, we actually got proactive about understanding our needs and then pursued an environment where we could thrive?

TWO VALUABLE INSIGHTS

I learned two things about gardening that day: first, know what a plant needs in order to flourish, and second, place each plant in its ideal environment.

The "bad" plants I bought for my yard were not really bad at all. They were simply struggling to make it in the wrong environment.

Maybe you've felt like those plants—stuck in an environment that doesn't fit who you were created to be. Maybe you're struggling, unable to flourish, and you don't know why.

You're not alone. I've felt that way too. Just as God designed different needs, he designed people with differing needs as well.

Let's explore how these gardening insights apply to our lives.

Insight One: Discover Who You Are

In landscaping terms, what type of "plant" are you? Are you aware of the unique gifts, talents, and competencies God has given you? Do you know what energizes you from within? Is your life passion clear to you? Does it compel you to give your very best? Are you clear on the unique contributions God created you to make in this world—and are you making them? Understanding who you are is essential for you to flourish.

Insight Two: Check Your Current Environment

When it comes to your life's mission, vocation, or calling, are you in the ideal environment to thrive? Does your current setting maximize your gifts, passion, and potential? Are you flourishing and fruitful?

To answer these questions, you must have a clear understanding of self. As you look at your self in the mirror, are you seeing what God sees? Or do you see what others have described, assumed, or pressured you to be? Until we know who God designed us to be, we can't possibly know what we need or how to get it. We won't have a clue about where we fit best or in what type of environment we will thrive.

A QUICK SELF-CHECK

Which of the following statements do you identify with?

☐ I'm capable of accomplishing more than I'm presently achieving.

☐ I sense God wants to use me in a meaningful way, but I'm not sure how or where.

☐ I feel frustrated and confused about my next steps. I'm not sure what to do with my life.

☐ I want to make a difference with my life, but I'm not as confident or competent as I think I should be.

☐ I'm not sure what I'm passionate about or what my purpose in life should be.

☐ It feels like everyone but me has life figured out—and I wonder what's wrong with me.

If you checked any of the statements above, then this book is for you. In the coming chapters, you'll find insights, tools, and assessments that will help you discover your unique, God-given gifts, relational style, and life passion. You'll gain practical insights into your self as you identify the person God made you to be. You'll discover ways you can build a life of greater significance, one that impacts others and honors God. You'll gain clarity about the sort of environment that helps you flourish. Then you'll put all this self-discovery into meaningful, tangible action so you can embrace the life God created you to live—a life of faith, fruitfulness, and fulfillment.

LOVING YOUR SELF

Jesus taught his followers to "love your neighbor as yourself."[2] In our desire to emphasize the importance of loving others, we sometimes overlook the underlying presumption in this command: we first must love our selves.

Loving our selves isn't about selfishness or arrogance. Godly self-love comes from a place of humility that acknowledges the deep value of all God's creations, including us. We can only love our selves fully when we understand how God's love created us. That understanding, in turn, makes it easier to love others, since he made them with the same purpose and care.

Your self as a person is a unique and valuable entity. If you don't truly know your self, how can you understand your purpose and the you-shaped contributions you can make?

As you invest time and intentionality in identifying *who* God made you to be, you'll begin to see more clearly *how* you can best love God, others, and your self. You'll be able to make decisions that better reflect your truest self, and those decisions will shape your life.

In years past, before I understood how God had created me, I often felt something must be wrong with me. No matter what role I held, I never quite felt like I was being my full self. Sure, I could deliver a satisfactory performance, but "good enough" wasn't good enough for me. I wasn't thriving. I knew there must be something more.

Once you've identified who you are and what type of environment you need, you'll be able to start living the life of significance God planned for you all along.

It wasn't until I began assessing how God purposefully created me—my gifts, passions, talents, spiritual gifts, and temperament—that I realized how important my environment was.

Our environment includes the people around us, the tasks we're responsible for, the different ways we can fulfill those tasks, the resources available to us, the feedback we receive, and the atmosphere, spirit, and teamwork that help us do what we do best.

Once you've identified who you are and what type of environment you need, you'll be able to start living the life of significance God planned for you all along.

NOT *IF* BUT *HOW* AND *WHERE*

Jesus modeled a life of significance and service throughout his years on earth, most overtly during the Last Supper, when he took a servant's towel and washed the dusty feet of his followers, a chore usually relegated to a servant.[3] He demonstrated the ultimate act of service when he gave his very life in our place through his death on the cross.

God invites us to join him in helping his will to "be done, on earth as it is in heaven."[4] We're called to serve both God and others—and deep down most of us truly want to do just that. Whether in our day jobs or in our volunteer roles in our community, we want to make a difference. The problem isn't in knowing *if* we should serve God and others; it's in knowing *how* and *where* to serve best.

The problem isn't in knowing if we should serve God and others; it's in knowing how and where to serve best.

We have two options:

1. Choose the trial-and-error method, in which we constantly replant our selves in different environments until we find one that fits (wasting valuable time and fighting discouragement along the way), or
2. Discover who God created us to be and get our selves planted in an environment that fits *how* and *where* we need to be—a place where we can thrive.

I've tried both options, and trust me: door #2 is much more efficient and rewarding! By reading this book, you're already demonstrating that you're choosing door #2.

FOCUSED PRAYER

Lord,
I really want to make a difference,
but I'm not sure how.
Give me the wisdom to know who you made me to be
and where I can best make a contribution.
Reveal to me my spiritual gifts,
my relational style,
and my life passion.
Most of all, give me a servant's heart.
Help me to seek your way,
make peace with my past,
and have confidence in my future.
Empower me to follow the example you've set.
Help me fulfill the unique purpose
you've designed for my life.
Show me the way.
Amen.

REFLECTION:
Questions for Journaling and Discussion

Use these questions to process and personalize what you've just read.

1. Do you agree or disagree with Bruce's distinction between "yourself" and "your self"? Do you feel it is a meaningful distinction? Why or why not?
2. Have you ever felt like a plant struggling to survive in the wrong environment? Describe your situation.
3. Imagine you were planted exactly where you could thrive and bear fruit as a follower of Jesus. What difference would it make to you? To others?
4. In the Quick Self-Check on page 7, which statement is most true of you right now? Explain.
5. How important is self-love in order to "love your neighbor as yourself"? What keeps you from having more self-love?
6. What is the one question you most hope this book will answer for you?

WHERE IS IT WRITTEN?
Scripture Passages for Further Study

For I am confident of this very thing, that He who began a good work among you will complete it by the day of Christ Jesus.

Philippians 1.6

Matthew 22.36–40   Ephesians 4.11–16

John 13.3–9   1 Peter 2.9–10

2 WHO DOES GOD SAY YOU ARE?

SEEING GOD'S PLAN:
The Potter and the Clay

Some people journey through life with the idea that God's plan for their life is sealed in a mysterious time capsule out there somewhere, and until they find it, they can't really know what God wants them to do. That search can feel like a cosmic game of hide-and-seek, which is not the type of relationship God has with us. The plan isn't "out there." The clues to God's plan are already within you. God put them there on purpose.

The Bible talks about a potter who works with clay, and everything the potter creates has a unique purpose.[1] First, the potter decides what to make, and then they begin to form the clay into its intended purpose.

A plate has a distinct purpose: to hold food.

A vase has a purpose: to hold water and flowers.

A cup has a purpose: to hold a beverage.

Like the clay, you also have a purpose. With a unique purpose in mind, God determined how to create you, giving you everything you need to be the best "you" possible. He formed you with gifts, personality, and passions so you can live a life filled with meaning, purpose, and significance. He created you to make a difference in your relationships, family, faith community, and work.

A FRESH PERSPECTIVE

When I was a kid, I liked to do those connect-the-dot puzzles. For me, they held a kind of mystery and intrigue. With pencil in hand, I would draw a line from one dot to the next, and slowly an image would appear. What at first looked like a bunch of dots on a page soon had meaning. Once I knew what the image was, it seemed obvious. How could I not have seen it?

Connecting dots can be quite informative. Try this exercise: See if you can connect the nine dots below with four straight lines without lifting your pen or pencil from the paper. Take a minute to try it. Don't give up. It really can be done.

Let me show you how it can be done.

1. Start at dot 1 and draw the first line downward. Move through dots 4 and 7, to the empty dot located below dot 7.
2. From that location, draw the second line diagonally, up and to the right, passing through dots 8 and 6, to the empty dot located to the right of dot 3.
3. From there, draw the third line back toward the left, passing through dots 3 and 2, ending up at dot 1.
4. Finally, draw the fourth and final line from dot 1 diagonally, downward and to the right, passing through dot 5 and ending at dot 9.

Four continuous straight lines, all dots connected.

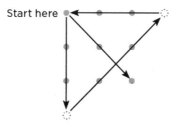

Start here

When most people try to solve this exercise, they can't figure it out because they limit their lines to the dots they can already see on the page. When shown the solution, they cry foul: "You didn't tell me I could draw outside the box! I didn't know it was okay to go beyond the lines."

What box? What lines?

When it comes to certain aspects of our lives, we often do the same thing. We live within nonexistent boxes or rules that keep us from accomplishing what we're meant to do. Perhaps our goal seems impossible because we've imposed imaginary boundaries or accepted limitations placed on us by others. We need to be open to the possibility that the rules we've adopted about who we are may be different from what is actually true.

In our early years, our parents shaped how we saw ourselves. Later in life, teachers, coaches, bosses, pastors, and other people of influence undoubtedly affected our self-perception as well. But no parent, boss, or pastor sees us with complete clarity. They can't. They're only human. God sees us clearly, and it's his perception we must seek.

> *No parent, boss, or pastor sees us with complete clarity. They can't. They're only human. God sees us clearly, and it's his perception we must seek.*

Our perspective not only affects how we see our selves; it defines the way we interpret and view those around us. The good news is we can enlarge our perspective to view things from God's vantage point—to see as God sees.

IN SEARCH OF A BIBLICAL PERSPECTIVE

People saw Peter as a common fisherman. Jesus saw Peter as a fisher of people.[2]

People saw Saul as a persecutor of the church. God saw him as Paul, an ambassador for the church.[3]

People saw Hannah as a woman who couldn't get pregnant and therefore must be cursed. God saw Hannah as a faith-filled woman who would give birth to Samuel, future judge in Israel.[4]

People saw David as a shepherd of sheep. God saw David as a shepherd of his people.[5]

The culture of the day saw Deborah as a second-class citizen because she was a woman. God saw Deborah as a judge, prophet, and mighty military leader.[6]

Gideon saw himself as the lowest person in his family's lineage. God saw Gideon as a powerful leader who would lead an army to defeat the enemies of his people.[7]

Moses saw himself as a criminal who was afraid to speak in public. God saw Moses as the one who would confront Pharaoh and lead God's people out of slavery.[8]

Mary saw herself as unworthy to be used by God. God saw Mary as the trusted mother of his one and only Son.[9]

John the Baptist knew he was not the Chosen One. God chose John to be the one who would prepare people for the One—Jesus, the Messiah.[10]

As I mentioned earlier, I did not see my self as a writer, but God saw me as an author with a message. And once I embraced God's vision of me, I became who he knew I could be.

God doesn't judge us by our gender, race, ethnicity, religion, physical abilities, or past failures. He sees us as his beloved children—his favored creations, filled with infinite potential.

How do you see your self? How does God see you? The Israelite judge Samuel answered that question this way: "The LORD does not look at the things people look at. People look at the outward appearance, but the LORD looks at the heart."[11]

For most of us, seeing as God sees requires a new way of thinking. We need a fresh perspective. Gaining a clear, biblical perspective helps us assess both the purpose of our life and our unique role within our relationships, vocation, and life's mission.

I challenge you to consider and reconsider how God sees you. Pray about it. Discuss it with safe, wise friends. Listen to what they say, to what they see in you, and to what God is revealing to you through their insights. We need God's help to see as he sees. As you listen for God's voice, you'll become more confident in his perspective.

> "The LORD does not look at the things people look at. People look at the outward appearance, but the LORD looks at the heart."
> 1 SAMUEL 16.7 NIV

God created you to fulfill vital needs in this world that you've been uniquely equipped and impassioned to fulfill. The apostle Paul put it this way: "We are God's handiwork, created in Christ Jesus to do good works, which God prepared in advance for us to do."[12]

You are free to "do good works" for those around you every day at home and in the office, classroom, or community. God calls you to be his hands and feet wherever you are. The options are limitless, and it's up to you to discover where God wants you to use the gifts you've been given.

Once you discover who God created you to be and then begin expressing your true identity, your personal, professional, and ministry contributions will take on new levels of purpose and meaning. Your influence will expand and your value to those around you will increase.

INVEST IN YOUR SELF: Five Commitments

God's purpose for your life is not a big mystery. As you explore your spiritual gifts, relational style, and passions in the coming chapters of this book, you'll discover your purpose. This process requires more than just reading. You'll need to put thought, time, and prayer into it. The real benefits come as you engage in personal reflection along the way.

Make this investment in your self. You're worth it.

Consider the statements below and initial the ones you can commit to throughout your journey.

1. _____ I commit to praying daily so I can better discern God's Spirit and be open to the truths he teaches me along the way.

2. _____ I commit to discovering my spiritual gifts so I can accomplish God's work in the world around me.

3. _____ I commit to utilizing my relational style as an important way God can relate to others through me.

4. _____ I commit to identifying the passions God has put into my heart so I can make a meaningful difference in this world.

5. _____ I commit to pursuing my purpose and an area of my calling so I can be faithful, fruitful, and fulfilled in the life God has given me to live.

FOCUSED PRAYER

Lord,
allow me to see this world through your eyes.
Teach me what your intentional design for me really means.
Thanks for revealing your purposeful perspectives
of me, of your church, of your creation.
Help me see myself as you do—
with a contribution to make,
a passion to pursue,
and enough faith to hear your voice—
and follow wherever you may lead.
In Jesus' name.
Amen.

REFLECTION:
Questions for Journaling and Discussion

1. A plate, cup, and fork are each designed to function differently. If you knew how you were designed, how might you function differently from others?
2. When you tried to connect the dots on page 14, did you succeed? What did you discover about your ability to break free from your assumptions?
3. Do you think it will be easy or hard to let go of some of your long-held self-perceptions? Explain.
4. Why is it important to know who God says you are?
5. As you begin this process of self-discovery, what are a few assumptions you have?
6. Which one of the commitments you made on page 18 will be the most challenging to keep? What can you do to strengthen your ability to keep that commitment?

WHERE IS IT WRITTEN?
Scripture Passages for Further Study

"The LORD does not look at the things people look at. People look at the outward appearance, but the LORD looks at the heart."   1 Samuel 16.7 NIV

Isaiah 29.16	Romans 9.21
Isaiah 45.9	Ephesians 2.10
Isaiah 64.8	

SECTION 2

THE EMERGING YOU

Spiritual Gifts

WHAT'S THE BIG DEAL ABOUT SPIRITUAL GIFTS?

D o spiritual gifts really matter? Is it really that important that we know which gifts God has given us and how best to deploy them?

Consider the words of Paul in his letter to the early church in Corinth: "Now concerning spiritual gifts, brothers and sisters, I do not want you to be unaware."[1]

It's an interesting choice of words. Paul issues a heads-up to his readers. It's almost a warning. And yet many Christ followers today— and many churches and leaders—don't really heed the alert Paul offers. They remain unaware or uninterested in the New Testament teachings regarding spiritual gifts.

Why do you think something so clearly stated is so widely ignored? Is it just easier to pursue what we want to do in life rather than investigate what God created and called us to do? Is it quicker for organizational leaders to tell staff and volunteers what they need to do? It takes an equipping leader to invest in others and empower them to make their unique contributions based on their God-given gifts and passions.

Spiritual gifts are not a Christian fad. They're not an arbitrary, subjective, ever-evolving list of nice skills we may or may not have. Rather, spiritual gifts are a distinct set of God-given abilities listed in Scripture that are strategically distributed to his people.

Your spiritual gifts are key indicators of your unique contribution and life purpose. They're embedded and are a part of your spiritual

DNA. Your gifts speak to your purpose and your desire to know where you belong.

Spiritual gifts are not a shift toward something new, but a return to what is original and foundational in the body of Christ. The establishment of the first church as told in Acts 2 was accomplished by the coming of the Holy Spirit and his work within the body of Christ through spiritual gifts that were distributed to each of its members.

God is still at work in the life of every individual who makes a decision to follow Christ. Through a movement of his Holy Spirit, God is entrusting his work into the hands of his followers. Christ followers discover their spiritual gifts and put them into practice.

The Great Commission

"Go and make disciples of all nations, baptizing them in the name of the Father and of the Son and of the Holy Spirit, and teaching them to obey everything I have commanded you. And surely I am with you always, to the very end of the age." MATTHEW 28.19-20 NIV

God is calling Christians *back* to being the biblical community of integrity the Holy Spirit first empowered Christ's disciples to be in Acts 2. By functioning in greater alignment with our spiritual gifts, we are more able to fulfill the Great Commission Jesus gave his followers in Matthew 28.19–20—to go and make a difference in the lives of others in his name.

A SPIRITUAL RECALIBRATION

The scale in your bathroom is designed to be a true indicator of your weight. Scales are set to zero by the factory, but because they can get out of adjustment, they're designed with the ability to be reset or recalibrated back to zero. If you're about to weigh yourself but you notice the needle is pointing to "4," you can simply reset it to "0" so you'll get an accurate read.

Today's focus on understanding the gifts is a spiritual recalibration, a resetting of the scale so we get an accurate reading on who we are. God wants each of us to rediscover his original plan so we can get back to pursuing his purpose for us and his church. This movement will not go away. It's part of God's original design.

BIBLICAL PERSPECTIVES ON SPIRITUAL GIFTS

Within the broad range of Christian theology, there can be differing viewpoints on some aspects of spiritual gifts. For the purpose of this book, allow me to articulate seven nonnegotiable, foundational truths as laid out clearly in Scripture.

1. God Wants Us to Know about the Spiritual Gifts

Now concerning spiritual gifts, brothers and sisters, I do not want you to be unaware.   *1 Corinthians 12.1*

"Spiritual gifts" in the original Greek text is a compound word. πνευματικῶν is a combination of πνευμα (spirit, spiritual) and τικῶν (gifts, things). The compound word would be translated "spiritual gifts" or "divine abilities."

There are varieties of gifts, but the same Spirit.

1 Corinthians 12.4

In this verse, "gifts" is another compound word in Greek: χαρις (divine grace) + μάτων (gifts) = "gifts of grace." A part of the grace we receive from God comes in the form of spiritual gifts. God is a grace giver, and by using our gifts for the benefit of others, we too can be grace givers.

2. God Wants Us to Know Our Unique Spiritual Gifts

To each one of us grace was given according to the measure of Christ's gift.

Ephesians 4.7

To each one is given the manifestation of the Spirit for the common good.

1 Corinthians 12:7

Since we have gifts that differ according to the grace given to us, each of us is to use them properly.

Romans 12.6

Since "each one" has received a spiritual gift, God intends for us to know what it is so we can fulfill the calling to which each of us has been called. Your gifts are the ways he empowers you to be effective, significant, and successful in his eyes.

3. God Wants Us to Use Our Spiritual Gifts

Do not neglect the spiritual gift within you.

1 Timothy 4.14

Each of you should use whatever gift you have received to serve others.

1 Peter 4.10 NIV

The Creator knows our need to be needed. He designed us with a longing to belong. In meeting the needs of others, we find the satisfaction of being connected with them. Our sense of belonging is validated by the mutual connection between grace givers (those able to meet a need) and grace receivers (those able to accept having their needs met by someone else).

4. God Chose the Specific Gifts His Holy Spirit Would Give Us in Order for Us to Fulfill Our Life's Purpose

One and the same Spirit works all these things, distributing to each one individually just as He wills.

1 Corinthians 12.11

Now God has arranged the parts, each one of them in the body, just as He desired. *1 Corinthians 12.18*

5. God Gave Us Spiritual Gifts to Use for the Benefit of Others

To each one is given the manifestation of the Spirit for the common good. *1 Corinthians 12.7*

We have been grace receivers so that we can be grace givers.

If we fail to use our gifts, we become grace robbers, withholding God's grace given to us for others. Our gifts are not *for* us but have been given *to* us for the benefit of others (the common good).

6. The Spiritual Gifts God Gave Us Are Permanent

The gifts and the calling of God are irrevocable.

Romans 11.29

7. God Expects Us to Manage and Develop Our Gifts

Each of you should use whatever gift you have received to serve others, as faithful stewards of God's grace in its various forms.

1 Peter 4.10 NIV

Our spiritual gifts are given to maximize and further God's kingdom in the world, and failing to use and develop those gifts is poor stewardship. We've been entrusted with priceless gifts, and God cares about how we manage such treasure.

These are some compelling reasons to be aware—not ignorant—of the spiritual gifts, and specifically *our* unique gifts.

Some believers fail to use their gifts as God intended out of ignorance. Others are aware but disobedient. Still others have not yet realized their purpose and identity in Christ—and are therefore unaware of how and where they can best use their gifts.

The New Testament likens the church to a physical body.[2] Drawing from this analogy, if a leg is not making its contribution, the body will limp, and over time the leg will atrophy and become ineffective and deformed. It won't be able to make its intended and significant contribution.

This means the rest of the body has to work extra hard to compensate for the inoperative leg. This compensation gives the body an unnatural gait and impaired function. It's clearly not the way the body was designed to function.

You are not merely needed; you've been created to contribute to a healthier whole—to build healthier communities, organizations, churches, and relationships.

Imagine a world in which all believers knew their spiritual gifts and were using them. Imagine the joy followers of Christ would experience as they made significant contributions to the world around them! Meaningful relationships and more fulfilling service to God and others would honor God, enrich communities, and transform lives.

Jesus tells this story:[3]

A generous boss left for an extended trip. He gave three of his employees some money to invest for him while he was away. One received ten thousand dollars; another, five thousand dollars; and the third, one thousand dollars.

When the boss returned, he summoned the three and asked them how they had done with the money he had entrusted to them. The first brought him twenty thousand dollars, saying he'd managed an investment portfolio and was able to double its net worth. The boss was pleased at how well this employee had done and told him how proud he was.

The second employee had much the same story to tell. She placed her boss's original five thousand dollars on the table plus five thousand more, which she had netted in a number of land transactions. The boss's pleasure was reflected on his face. "Well done," he said.

By this time, the third employee was feeling a little embarrassed. With a mixture of fear and pride in his voice, he explained how he had taken the thousand dollars and put it in his safe. "That way no one would find or steal it," he explained. Then he returned to the boss his original one thousand dollars.

The boss was visibly surprised and disappointed by the man's actions. An uncomfortable silence followed, and the man squirmed. "You would have been upset if I had invested the money and lost it," he rationalized.

"That being true," the boss replied, "why didn't you at least put the money in the bank to draw simple interest?"

The employee was fired for neglecting to manage what had been entrusted to him and for failing be a good steward of vital resources.

Jesus' point is clear: God expects a return on his investment. Someday we will give an account for the resources he entrusted to us. He wants us to be good stewards or managers of our spiritual gifts in a way that honors him and improves the lives of others.

When we're living this kind of life, it feels good. It feels peaceful. It feels right—and for good reason: spiritual gifts come with benefits. In the next chapter, we'll look at some of the powerful benefits that spiritual gifts add to our lives.

FOCUSED PRAYER

Lord,
thank you for so generously giving spiritual gifts
to everyone who belongs to you
through Jesus Christ.
Help me to better understand
what those gifts mean to me
and how I can use them the way you want me to.
Help me to please you by being a good manager of my gifts,
using them to bless the people in my life and beyond.
Help me to be an active participant in your purposes.
Open my eyes, Lord,
and reveal the gifts you have given me
so I can honor you
by making an impact in this world.
Amen.

REFLECTION:
Questions for Journaling or Discussion

1. What do you see as the greatest benefit of spiritual gifts? Explain.
2. If you had to give an account to God today for how you have used your spiritual gift(s) in your life so far, what would you say?
3. How is your community being affected by those who are using their spiritual gifts? By those who are not?
4. "If we fail to use our gifts, we become grace robbers." Do you agree or disagree? Explain.
5. In terms of fulfilling your life's purpose, what does it mean to you to know your gifts are permanent (that is, irrevocable)?

WHERE IS IT WRITTEN?
Scripture Passages for Further Study

The gifts and the calling of God are irrevocable.

Romans 11.29

Matthew 25.14–30   Ephesians 4.11–16
Acts 2.42—44   1 Timothy 4.14
Romans 12.1   1 Peter 4.8–11
1 Corinthians 12

THE BENEFITS OF SPIRITUAL GIFTS

DESCRIPTION OF SPIRITUAL GIFTS

God has been clear about the importance of identifying and using our spiritual gifts. Before we go any further, let's unpack a working description of a spiritual gift: *A spiritual gift is a God-given ability distributed by the Holy Spirit to every believer according to God's design for the common good of his people.*

Let's take a closer look:

A spiritual gift is a God-given ability . . . Gifts are specific skills God gives us that enable us to make our unique contributions in this world. They are not natural talents; they are divine abilities that give our lives purpose and honor him.

> *A spiritual gift is a God-given ability distributed by the Holy Spirit to every believer according to God's design for the common good of his people.*

. . . distributed by the Holy Spirit . . . These divine abilities are given to us by God's grace when we receive Jesus by trusting him for the forgiveness of our sins and becoming a part of the body of Christ. The Holy Spirit distributes gifts and empowers their use, equipping us to make meaningful contributions for his kingdom purposes.

. . . to every believer according to God's design . . . There is no Christ follower without a spiritual gift. Every believer has at least one spiritual gift. Gifts are part of God's design for our lives and equip us to fulfill his purposes according to that design.

. . . for the common good of his people. Our spiritual gift is not for ourselves; it's given to us to benefit others. Our divine ability enables us to meet a need in someone else's life. It empowers us to serve one another better. Gifts equip us to have an impact on God's kingdom and make a lasting difference in the lives of others in our church, community, mission, and marketplace.

BENEFITS OF SPIRITUAL GIFTS

Using your spiritual gifts has personal, relational, and kingdom benefits. Let's take a closer look.

Personal Benefits

Once you discover and begin using your spiritual gifts, you begin fulfilling your spiritual job description.

If you're committed to fulfilling God's purposes for your life but aren't yet certain what spiritual gifts you have, you'll want to do a careful assessment (we'll talk about that shortly). God has called you and given you the appropriate gifts to fulfill that calling. By knowing and using your gifts accordingly, you will be better able to accomplish his purposes.

Your gifts make things pretty clear. They'll show you the types of activities you should be doing:

> If God gave you the spiritual gift of encouragement, he wants you to come alongside others and encourage them.
> If God gave you the spiritual gift of teaching, he wants you to deliver relevant and timely truths by teaching individuals or groups.
> If God gave you the spiritual gift of helps, he wants you to help others by assisting them in their tasks.

Your life's purpose becomes more focused once you know your spiritual job description. It's easy to slip into saying yes to activities at the expense of your specific and primary contribution; your spiritual gift helps you determine the best expression of your self—and knowing what things to say yes to makes it much easier to say no to things that better fit someone else's spiritual gifting.

> Therefore, I urge you, brothers and sisters, in view of God's mercy, to offer your bodies as a living sacrifice, holy and pleasing to God—this is your true and proper worship. Do not conform to the pattern of this world, but be transformed by the renewing of your mind. Then you will be able to test and approve what God's will is—his good, pleasing and perfect will. *Romans 12.1–2 NIV*

Does this mean we should say no to things solely because they wouldn't allow us to use our primary spiritual gifts? Of course not. God calls all of us to be generous even if giving isn't a primary spiritual gift. He calls all of us to share our faith with others even if evangelism isn't at the top of our gift list. Your best energies should be invested in your primary gifts, but that's not an excuse to hold back in areas God asks all of us to contribute to as Christ followers. Lean into your primary gifts and occasionally contribute to other areas as well.

Expressing the gifts of the Spirit is viewed by God as an act of spiritual worship. Serving through your giftedness pleases God and reveals his purpose for you personally. It identifies your role. Once you know and use your spiritual gifts, you'll be well on the path toward becoming more faithful, fruitful, and fulfilled.

Jesus told his followers, "My Father is glorified by this, that you bear much fruit, and so prove to be My disciples."[1] God's intention is that we bear fruit. Like the two faithful employees in Jesus' story I shared earlier, we're to be responsible stewards of our gifts and invest them diligently.

Using our spiritual gifts helps us be faithful to the calling of God on our lives. As we become faithful in using our gifts, we'll become more fruitful, seeing the kind of results that honor God and benefit others.

Jesus goes on to tell his followers, "These things I have spoken to you so that My joy may be in you, and that your joy may be made full."[2] Not only does Jesus invite us to be faithful and fruitful by using our gifts, but he also anticipates that as a result, we'll feel fulfilled. We will experience the kind of deep joy that comes only from doing something that we were made to do—and knowing that God designed us specifically for that purpose.

When we're serving others through the faithful stewardship of our spiritual gifts, our lives and ministry experiences bring greater personal satisfaction because we know we're making a kingdom difference—and are making God known through our lives and beyond.

RELATIONAL BENEFITS

People and ministries that teach and function according to the spiritual gifts experience more unity and harmony.

Confusion and disharmony can't help but exist among believers when there is a lack of appreciation for the unique contributions each individual is to make through their God-given gifts. People's differences are not obstacles for God. Rather, he views them as opportunities for us to serve one another in a variety of ways, meeting one another's diverse needs.

Have you been in a meeting where one person seemed deeply concerned about who was to do what by when? Some might assume they're just an uptight worrier, but it could actually be their gift of administration showing itself and seeking to bring order to a chaotic task (a much-needed organizational contribution, by the way!).

Perhaps someone else is preoccupied with checking in on the neediest person in the group—the one who seems most worried or upset. That person's gift of mercy could be making a needed contribution by tending to that hurting individual.

Maybe you notice the person sitting across from you loses interest when the conversation takes a visionary, big-picture turn. They just wish someone would give them a list of the tasks that need to get done.

Their gift of helps wants to assist others by getting the practical tasks completed—another vital contribution.

Finally, maybe you observe that the person running the meeting is in their element as the group discusses the next big project. They masterfully guide the conversation, drawing from the wisdom of each person in the room while keeping the focus on the big picture. Their gift of leadership is having a field day, and everyone else relaxes in the presence of their leadership skills.

Each person at that meeting fulfills a different—but equally vital—role. They each make contributions that God designed them to make. This is how spiritual gifts are meant to function. We need each other. We need the gifts of each individual.

When I hear and see these kinds of behaviors in a group meeting, I thank God for his gifts and count my blessings that he's placed me among people who have spiritual gifts that are different from mine. I appreciate each person's contribution with greater understanding and deeper gratitude. And this is exactly as God planned it:

> God placed all things under his feet and appointed him to be head over everything for the church . . .
>
> Then we will no longer be infants . . . Instead, speaking the truth in love, we will grow to become in every respect the mature body of him who is the head, that is, Christ. From him the whole body, joined and held together by every supporting ligament, grows and builds itself up in love, as each part does its work.
>
> *Ephesians 1.22; 4.14–16 NIV*

Jesus, as the head of the church (the body of Christ), has designed each member of his body to function in ways that complement the others and meet the diverse variety of needs within it.

Identifying and using our spiritual gifts clarifies God's purposes for us. It makes us less inclined to see our differences as obstacles. We can function as complementary parts rather than as competitors.

COMMUNITY BENEFITS

People, teams, ministries, and organizations that teach about spiritual gifts and truly function accordingly will exhibit less pride and have a greater impact.

When we don't understand spiritual gifts, we are much more likely to take personal credit for our accomplishments. Spiritual pride can emerge.

Spiritual pride often shows itself through frequent use of such phrases as:

"I did . . ."
"Did you see what I . . . ?"
"I'm going to . . ."
"I'm telling you, I . . ."
"I . . . I . . . I . . ."

At the other end of the spectrum are those who practice a kind of false humility. They like to say others clearly have a spiritual gift, but they, unfortunately, do not. These types of people take the position of a humble servant who is unable to do anything worthwhile. They say, "I can't sing like Alejandro, I can 't lead like Brie, and I can't teach like Logan, so I'll just help out wherever I can."

They may sound like they're being humble, but in fact they're demonstrating false humility. Every person has a vital contribution to make by using their God-given gifts.

Let's keep it real. If you don't know what your gift is or where or how to use it, it may be easy to conclude you don't have a spiritual gift, but that simply isn't true. As we have seen, every follower of Christ has at least one spiritual gift.

Both spiritual pride and false humility are the result of ignorance about the topic of spiritual gifts. Once we've examined what Scripture has to say about gifts and have begun using our gifts to benefit others and honor God, we dramatically lower our level of spiritual pride because we know whatever fruit we see as a result of our actions stems from the gift God gave us. It's not from our own efforts or talents (though we must cooperate and be willing to be used by God in this way). We gain a true and accurate understanding of God's power and purposes.

For those stuck in false humility, some sound teaching about spiritual gifts will elevate their ownership of their gifts and their responsibility for using them to make a meaningful contribution. Once informed, they move from being disinterested observers to purposeful participants. When this happens, ownership soars and we all benefit.

Teams, ministries, churches, and organizations that teach and develop the spiritual gifts stand out. Their people demonstrate growth and maturity.

When parts of the physical body don't function properly or don't function at all, the body fails to develop and mature as needed. Infants depend on their livers, lungs, hearts, kidneys, and other vital organs to function properly in order to experience normal growth and development. If one, two, or more parts of the body fail to operate, the body is unable to hear, walk, or perhaps even breathe.

> *Once informed, they move from being disinterested observers to purposeful participants.*

As each part of the body makes its appropriate contribution, the body gets stronger and grows to maturity. An infant grows to be an adult and hopefully a contributing member of society.

The same is true for the people of God. It is through the proper functioning of spiritual gifts that the body of Christ grows healthy and strong: "Now you are the body of Christ, and each one of you is a part of it."[3]

A good question to ask yourself is this: *Am I doing my part and making my appropriate contribution to the body?*

KINGDOM BENEFIT

God is honored and people benefit when we teach and develop gift-based ministries.

God is pleased when the gifts he has given are used to honor him in ministering to others.

Jesus told his followers, "You are the light of the world . . . Let your light shine before others that they may see your good deeds and glorify your Father in heaven."[4] When our spiritual gifts are properly expressed, people can more readily see our motivation to serve others. They recognize that our acts of servanthood can only be the result of a heart that has been truly transformed by a loving, gracious, and caring God. In short, God gets the credit, which is as it should be.

Spiritual gifts are for the common good, and they enable us to be faithful, fruitful, and fulfilled as we use them for God's purposes. They make God known to those who see our service in action. Spiritual gifts give us purpose as the Holy Spirit gives us power to honor God and benefit others.

Now that you have a better understanding of the role and purpose of spiritual gifts, it's time to get specific. In the next chapter, you'll begin the process of learning about each gift and identifying the one(s) God has given you.

FOCUSED PRAYER

Lord,
thank you for the love you have shown me
through the spiritual gifts you gave,
for the ways you keep on giving to me,
and for the benefits you provide.
Help me fulfill my spiritual job description
and bring more harmony to my relationships
and greater unity to the ministries, teams, and organizations
where you've placed me.
Help me recognize the times I take credit
for your work in my life,
and forgive me.
Help me to walk with confidence and true humility.
I want to honor you by being
faithful to how you have made me,
fruitful with the gifts you have given me,
and fulfilled by the purposes you have given me.
In Jesus name.
Amen.

REFLECTION:
Questions for Journaling or Discussion

1. In this chapter, a spiritual gift is described as "a God-given ability distributed by the Holy Spirit to every believer according to God's design for the common good of his people." What part of this description most encourages you? What part creates the greatest challenge?

2. If you really knew your spiritual gift(s) with absolute clarity, how might you be more focused to pursue its expression in your life?

3. When it comes to using spiritual gifts, in what ways does spiritual pride or false humility evidence itself in your life? What can you do to counter these temptations?

4. How would you answer the question posed on page 41: *Am I doing my part and making my appropriate contribution to the body?*

5. What has been your greatest learning or insight from these first four chapters?

WHERE IS IT WRITTEN?
Scripture Passages for Further Study

I . . . urge you to walk in a manner worthy of the calling with which you have been called. Ephesians 4.1

Matthew 5.13–16	John 15.11 (fulfilled)
Matthew 25.14–30	Romans 12.1–2
(faithful)	1 Corinthians 12.27
John 15.8 (fruitful)	

5 YOU'VE GOT GIFTS!

THE ANIMAL SCHOOL

It wasn't too long after creation that the animals got together to form a school. They wanted it to be the best school possible—one that offered its students a well-rounded curriculum of swimming, running, climbing, and flying. In order to graduate, all the animals had to take all the courses.

The duck was excellent at swimming. In fact, he was better than his instructor. But he was only making passing grades in climbing and was getting a very poor grade in running. The duck was so slow in running that he had to stay after school to practice running. His webbed feet got so sore from running that he became average in swimming. But average was quite acceptable to everyone, so no one worried much about it—except the duck.

The rabbit was at the top of her class in running. But after a while, she developed a twitch in her leg from all the time she spent in the water trying to improve her swimming.

The squirrel was a peak performer in climbing but was constantly frustrated in flying class. When jumping from the top of the tree, his body became so bruised from all the hard landings that it affected his climbing ability, and he ended up being pretty poor in running as well.

The eagle was a real problem student. She was continually called out for being a nonconformist because in climbing class, she always beat everyone else to the top of the tree but insisted on using her own way to get there.[1]

Each of the animals had a particular area of expertise. When they did what they were designed to do, they excelled. When they tried to operate outside their area of expertise, they were not nearly as effective. They became frustrated and discouraged.

Can ducks run? Sure they can. Is that what they do best? Definitely not.

PEOPLE WHO EXCEL

Just as each of those animals have an area in which they excel, so do God's people. Each of us has become a new creation in Christ.[2] Part of becoming that new creation is receiving spiritual gifts from God. Our gifts enable us. As we learn to use them, we begin to realize our full potential. Your gift indicates the role, function, or particular way in which God intends you to best serve and excel.

Let's explore what the various spiritual gifts are and how you can know your spiritual gift.

WHAT ARE THE SPIRITUAL GIFTS?

Many studies have been done and books have been written about spiritual gifts. While there is general agreement on the role and nature of the gifts, most of the studies vary to some degree in their specific lists of the gifts and their descriptions.

Several passages in Scripture mention specific spiritual gifts. I have listed the gifts from these passages, as well as a few passages that refer to additional gifts. Through a brief study of these gifts, you will see more clearly the unique way God desires us to serve him and others.

Primary Passages on Spiritual Gifts

Romans 12.6–8	Ephesians 4.1–16
1 Corinthians 12.8–10; 12.28	1 Peter 4.9–10

As you read about the gifts, reflect on your own experiences. Where do you naturally excel? Which spiritual gift might this indicate?

There is no right or wrong spiritual gift. No one gift is more valuable than another. Each gift is vital for the healthy functioning of the body of Christ, and each gift is unique. The nuances of how each individual stewards their gift add further dimension and originality.

Before you go online to take your Spiritual Gifts Assessment, spend a few minutes reading through the list of spiritual gifts and their brief descriptions in the table that follows. Ask yourself, *Does this gift describe me?* Then indicate your gut response by marking Definitely Yes, Definitely No, or Maybe/Unsure.

Definitely Yes	Maybe/ Unsure	Definitely No	Spiritual Gift	Description
			Administration	The God-given ability to understand what makes an organization function, and the special ability to plan and execute procedures that accomplish the goals of the ministry
			Apostleship	The God-given ability to start and oversee the development of new churches or ministry structures
			Craftsmanship	The God-given ability to creatively design and/or construct items to be used for ministry
			Creative Communication	The God-given ability to communicate God's truth through a variety of art forms
			Discernment	The God-given ability to distinguish between truth and error and to discern the spirits, differentiating between good and evil, right and wrong

(continued)

Definitely Yes	Maybe/ Unsure	Definitely No	Spiritual Gift	Description
			Encouragement	The God-given ability to present truth so as to strengthen, comfort, or urge to action those who are discouraged or wavering in their faith
			Evangelism	The God-given ability to effectively communicate the gospel to unbelievers so they respond in faith and move toward discipleship
			Faith	The God-given ability to act on God's promises with confidence and unwavering belief in his ability to fulfill his purposes
			Giving	The God-given ability to contribute money and resources to the work of the Lord with cheerfulness and liberality
			Healing	The God-given ability to be God's means for restoring people to wholeness
			Helps	The God-given ability to attach spiritual value to the accomplishment of practical and necessary tasks that free up, support, and meet the needs of others
			Hospitality	The God-given ability to care for people by providing a safe place for them to belong, connect, and be valued
			Intercession	The God-given ability to consistently pray on behalf of and for others, thus seeing frequent and specific results
			Interpretation	The God-given ability to make known to the body of Christ the message of one who is speaking in tongues

(continued)

Definitely Yes	Maybe/ Unsure	Definitely No	Spiritual Gift	Description
			Knowledge	The God-given ability to bring truth to the body through a revelation or biblical insight
			Leadership	The God-given ability to cast vision, motivate, and direct people to harmoniously accomplish the purposes of God
			Mercy	The God-given ability to cheerfully and practically help those who are suffering or in need
			Miracles	The God-given ability to authenticate the ministry and message of God through supernatural intervention that glorifies God
			Prophecy	The God-given ability to reveal truth and proclaim it in a timely and relevant manner for understanding, correction, repentance, or edification
			Shepherding	The God-given ability to nurture, care for, and guide people toward ongoing spiritual maturity and Christlikeness
			Teaching	The God-given ability to understand, clearly explain, and apply the Word of God, thus causing greater Christlikeness in the lives of listeners
			Tongues	The God-given ability to speak, worship, or pray in a language unknown to the speaker
			Wisdom	The God-given ability to apply spiritual truth effectively to meet a need in a specific situation

Isn't it amazing how many different ways God has uniquely empowered his people?

WHAT ARE YOUR SPIRITUAL GIFTS?

Now it's time to take the Spiritual Gifts Assessment to better understand the gifts God has given you. If you don't have access to the online assessments, they are also provided at the back of this book on page 179. Follow the instructions there to complete each assessment as it is assigned.

> To SET UP your online RIGHT4 YOU Profile:
> - Go to www.brucebugbee.com/profiles.
> - Follow the instructions to create your account and use the registration code: R4U.
>
> To RETURN to your RIGHT4 YOU Profile:
> - Go to www.brucebugbee.com/profiles.
> - Follow the instructions to access your account with username and password.
>
> BONUS MATERIAL! Get a *free* one-page description of each of the twenty-three spiritual gifts. Just click "Gift Descriptions" at www.brucebugbee.com/profiles.

Online Assessment #1: Spiritual Gifts

The purchase price of this book includes access to three online assessments:[3]

- Assessment #1: Spiritual Gifts
- Assessment #2: Relational Style
- Assessment #3: Life Passion

If you wish, you may write your log-in information at the back of the book on page 179 for easy reference.

For now, set aside about forty-five minutes of uninterrupted time and complete only the Spiritual Gifts Assessment. Resist the temptation to take all three assessments now. You will be invited to take the next two assessments later in the book, but your responses will be more accurate once you have an idea of each assessment's purpose.

After you've completed your Spiritual Gifts Assessment, click "Print Results" so you'll have a hard copy of your results on hand.[4] You may also want to print out the Gifts Descriptions document on that page for future reference. On page 180 you'll find a blank template titled "My RIGHT4 YOU Profile." There you'll be able to add each element of your unique profile as you work your way through the book.

You've just completed the first element of your RIGHT4 YOU Profile—your spiritual gifts. You can also download more details on each of the spiritual gifts. Read about your top three gifts and list a couple of new insights that will help you better understand those gifts. Write your top three spiritual gifts here:

1. _____
2. _____
3. _____

Your online results will look something like this:

YOUR SPIRITUAL GIFTS

You appear to reflect the following spiritual gifts:

Creative
Communication

Teaching

Shepherding

Mercy

Leadership

YOUR GIFT MIX

While every believer has at least one spiritual gift, many have several gifts. We refer to this as a gift mix. The combination of these gifts equips us to make nuanced contributions in a variety of situations.

Take a look at the gift mixes below to see how a specific combination of gifts works synergistically.

Sample Gift Mix #1: Mercy, Encouragement, Hospitality

If these are your gifts, they indicate a warm and tender expression of God's grace. You are able to focus on the lonely, forgotten, and needy people around you with the connecting and belonging inclinations of hospitality, along with the motivating and comforting aspects of encouragement. You value, support, and build the confidence and self-esteem of those around you. The nuanced expression of this gift mix serves others well.

Sample Gift Mix #2: Administration, Leadership, Wisdom

If these are your gifts, they indicate a strong ability to identify what needs to be done and to articulate the best way to do it. The systematic approach of administration plus the visionary dimensions of leadership enable you to move people and events forward. Others will benefit from the clarity and practicality of your commonsense approaches. The combination of these gifts adds dimension and impact over a singular gift alone.

Reflect on your spiritual gift mix from your RIGHT4 YOU Profile page 180). Describe a few times you've experienced an interactive expression of your gift mix.

_____

_____

_____

FOCUSED PRAYER

Lord,
thank you for the amazing array of gifts
you have poured out upon your people.
And thank you for giving me a specific spiritual gift
so I can contribute to this world
according to your perfect plan.
Help me recognize and embrace my gift.
If I have ignored it, forgive me.
If I have suppressed it, stir it up.
Direct my thoughts toward an area of service
that will utilize my gift,
and empower me to become everything
you created me to be—
fruitful, joyful, loving, faithful, and grateful.
Amen.

REFLECTION:
Questions for Journaling or Discussion

1. What did you most identify with in "The Animal School" story on page 45? Explain.
2. In your opinion, why does God want us to excel?
3. What word(s) best describes how you felt when you saw the results of your Spiritual Gifts Assessment?

__ Affirmed	__ Guilty	__ Other:
__ Surprised	__ Embarrassed	_____
__ Confused	__ Frustrated	
__ Excited	__ Disappointed	

4. How accurate do you think your gift results are? *Circle the number.*

Nope, not accurate   Nailed it!

1   2   3   4   5   6   7   8   9   10

5. Share your top gifts with someone who knows you well, and ask them, "From what you know of me, do you think these might be my spiritual gifts?" What did they say?

Nope, not accurate   Nailed it!

1   2   3   4   5   6   7   8   9   10

WHERE IS IT WRITTEN?
Scripture Passages for Further Study

One and the same Spirit works all these things, distributing to each one individually just as He wills.

1 Corinthians 12.11

Exodus 31.3-5	1 Corinthians 12.8-11, 28
Psalm 150.3-5	Ephesians 4.11
Romans 12.6-8	1 Peter 4.9-10

6 WHAT SPIRITUAL GIFTS ARE *NOT*

U p to this point, we have been focusing on what spiritual gifts are. For further clarity, let's look at four things spiritual gifts are *not*.

1. SPIRITUAL GIFTS ARE NOT NATURAL TALENTS

Everyone was born with some natural abilities, but God gives his spiritual gifts to believers at the time they receive his Holy Spirit and start following Christ. Let's compare and contrast natural talents and spiritual gifts.

A. Both Natural Talents and Spiritual Gifts Are God-Given

Natural talents and spiritual gifts both need to be identified, developed, and put to good use in order to fulfill our life's purpose and honor God.

B. Natural Talents Are Given at Our Physical Birth; Spiritual Gifts Are Given at Our Spiritual Birth

Just as we have distinct natural talents from birth that distinguish us from others, we receive one or more spiritual gifts that distinguish us from others when we are born spiritually and become Christ followers.[1] These gifts enable us to make our unique kingdom contributions.

C. Natural Talents Are an Expression of God's Common Grace; Spiritual Gifts Are an Expression of His Specific Grace

All humans, regardless of their faith (or lack of faith), were created by God and hold a measure of his grace, as evidenced by their natural talents. God gives an additional measure of grace to believers, evidenced by the spiritual gifts that equip them for advancing God's message and ministry. Both talents and gifts are designed to honor God and enrich the lives of others.

D. Natural Talents Can Sometimes—but Not Always— Partner Well with One's Spiritual Gifts

For example, someone may be an effective hospice nurse and also be recognized as having a mercy gift in the church. A graphic designer in the workplace may discover that they also have a spiritual gift of creative communication. And the successful salesperson may also have the gift of evangelism.

Often, however, there is no direct correlation between natural talents and spiritual gifts.

Being a teacher in the public school system does not necessarily mean the person has a spiritual gift of teaching. Being an effective manager in the marketplace does not guarantee anointed leadership or administration gifts.

To determine whether there is a correlation between your natural talents and a spiritual gift, ask yourself, *Does my natural ability regularly honor God and build up others in my circles at work, in my neighborhood, and in my faith community?*

E. Both Natural Talents and Spiritual Gifts Can Vary in Degree and in Kind

Some basketball players exhibit tremendous natural athletic ability, while others have to work incredibly hard just to play a little above average. Some singers' voices are pretty good, while others' voices are naturally great. Some with the spiritual gift of leadership will lead small groups of tens, while others may lead hundreds or even thousands. Some with the gift of helps use their gift in predictable ways each time, while others with the same gift prefer to help in a variety of ways and situations.

Each one of us is a steward or manager, responsible for all God has given us. Our talents and spiritual gifts are specific ways God has extended his grace to us so we can pass that grace on to others and bless them.

The chart below summarizes the relationship between natural talents and spiritual gifts.

	Natural Talents	Spiritual Gifts
A	God-given	God-given
B	Given at physical birth	Given at spiritual birth
C	God's common grace	God's specific grace
D	Sometimes a talent can be transformed by the Holy Spirit	May or may not correlate to a person's natural talents
E	Vary in degree and kind: Athlete Manager Musician Carpenter Etc.	Vary in degree and kind: Administration Leadership Creative Communication Craftsmanship Etc.

2. SPIRITUAL GIFTS ARE NOT THE FRUIT OF THE SPIRIT

The apostle Paul includes a list of Christlike attributes in his letter to the churches in Galatia. He calls these attributes "fruit of the Spirit": "The fruit of the Spirit is love, joy, peace, patience, kindness, goodness, faithfulness, gentleness, self-control."[2]

Both spiritual gifts and the fruit of the Spirit are necessary for us to be productive and fulfilled in our life, ministry, and work, but they make very different and distinct contributions.

A. The Fruit of the Spirit Are "Being" Qualities; Spiritual Gifts Are "Doing" Qualities

Fruit of the Spirit are inner characteristics of the believer's heart, revealed in their character as they grow and mature spiritually. The fruit of the Spirit indicate *how we should be*.

Spiritual gifts are "doing" qualities. They are task-oriented functions or roles that God has called and equipped each believer to perform. Spiritual gifts indicate *what we should do.*

B. The Fruit of the Spirit Reflect Attitudes; Spiritual Gifts Reflect Aptitudes

Have you ever been criticized for doing the right thing the wrong way? Our attitudes toward God and others greatly affect the impact of our aptitudes. We can pride ourselves on doing something with excellence, but if people distance themselves from us or our contribution because of our attitude, what have we accomplished?

The opposite is just as true. If people adore us because of our Christlike attitude but we're not making a meaningful contribution to this world, people notice over time a disconnect between how we act and what we actually do. This, too, will create relational distance.

A humble and teachable heart that reflects the fruit of the Spirit increases the impact of our actions.

C. The Fruit of the Spirit Are Byproducts; Spiritual Gifts Are Given

The fruit grow out of a close, enduring, and obedient relationship with Jesus Christ. Spiritual gifts are imparted to us by the Holy Spirit when we become Christians, and they are forever a part of us as we walk with God throughout our lives. As the apostle Paul writes, "God's gifts and his call are irrevocable."[3]

D. Both the Fruit of the Spirit and Gifts of the Spirit Are Essential for Our Life's Purpose and Ministry Effectiveness

Sometimes people wonder which are more important—the gifts or the fruit. This is like asking, "Which wing of an airplane is more important?" Both are essential!

If you have spiritual gifts given by the Holy Spirit but don't use them in a spirit of love and joy, they cannot accomplish the purposes for which God gave them to you. The apostle Paul writes, "If I have the gift of [name of a gift] . . . but do not have love, I am nothing."[4]

Likewise, if we demonstrate attitudes that reflect the fruit of the Spirit but are not doing the things the Holy Spirit gifted us to do, what good is it? Jesus' brother James describes it this way: "Just as the body without the spirit is dead, so also faith without works is dead."[5]

To maximize our impact in this world and our God-given purpose in life, we need to demonstrate both the fruit of the Spirit and the gifts of the Spirit.

	Fruit of the Spirit	Gifts of the Spirit
A	"Being" qualities	"Doing" qualities
B	Attitudes	Aptitudes
C	Byproduct of a healthy walk with God	Supernatural endowment of the Spirit
D	Essential for life's purpose and ministry effectiveness	Essential for life's purpose and ministry effectiveness

3. SPIRITUAL GIFTS ARE NOT SPIRITUAL PRACTICES

To develop and grow in Christlikeness, each of us needs to engage in regular practices—sometimes called disciplines—that keep us spiritually and relationally healthy. These hallmark practices are habits taught and modeled throughout Scripture and throughout history. Spiritual practices are evidenced in the life of every fully devoted follower of Christ.

Examples include prayer, study of Scripture, solitude, worship, fasting, journaling, a lifestyle of simplicity, acts of service, meditation, and sacrificial giving, to name a few.

A. Spiritual Practices Are Personal and Interpersonal Activities Designed to Strengthen the Individual; Spiritual Gifts Are Designed to Strengthen Others

Spiritual practices draw believers closer to God and help them grow in spiritual maturity and Christlikeness. These disciplines lead us to more intimately worship the majesty of God; to more clearly hear his voice, understand his Word, discern his will, and receive his Spirit's power; and to more consistently be nurtured in his love—all of which better equips us to use our spiritual gifts to extend his grace to others.

B. Spiritual Practices Are Some of the Many Ways We Connect with God and Build Relational Intimacy with Him; Spiritual Gifts Are the Specific Ways We Reflect God to Others and Build Up His People

Spiritual practices can take us deeper into the heart and mind of God. They help us be with Jesus in order to become like Jesus.

Exercising spiritual practices or using our spiritual gifts isn't a guarantee we will become godlier. However, both of these activities can lead us toward godliness and greater faithfulness to the people and purposes God has called us to. In Paul's letter to his young protégé Timothy, he emphasizes the importance of being spiritually disciplined: "Discipline yourself for the purpose of godliness."[6]

	Spiritual Practices	Spiritual Gifts
A	Activities designed to strengthen the individual	Activities designed to strengthen others
B	A means to connect with God and build relational intimacy with him	A means to reflect God to others and build up his people
	Examples:	*Examples:*
	Prayer	Intercession
	Study	Knowledge
	Fasting	Mercy
	Develops inner devotion	Makes a contribution to others
	What we do for the purpose of godliness	What we do for the purpose of a kingdom contribution

4. SPIRITUAL GIFTS ARE NOT POSITION TITLES

Positions we hold at work or as volunteers may or may not describe or align with our spiritual gifts. There is not necessarily a one-to-one correspondence between the way we function in a position or role and the skill set or spiritual gifts required to be successful in that role. Assuming they are the same creates confusion.

A. Titles Indicate General Roles; Spiritual Gifts Indicate Specific Functions

Those who hold the position of a small group *leader* may or may not have a spiritual gift of leadership. They may be leading primarily through their spiritual gift of encouragement, teaching, or hospitality. This is perfectly acceptable if they don't confuse their role with the gifts they may be using in that role.

B. Titles Indicate Organizational Positions; Spiritual Gifts Indicate Ministry Contributions

Every organization—even a small team—has some sort of hierarchical structure, usually with a leader at the top and then layers of various roles branching out from the top down. When we confuse spiritual gifts with position titles, we can create unhelpful expectations for those serving in leadership positions.

When it comes to how you function in your role(s) at work or in a volunteer position, knowing your spiritual gift helps immensely. It gives you clarity about how you'll function most effectively within whatever organizational position you hold.

	Position Titles	Spiritual Gifts
A	General roles	Specific functions
B	Title of organizational positions	Ministry contributions
	Examples:	*Examples:*
	Board member	Leadership
	Small group leader	Shepherding, Teaching
	Building and Grounds team	Helps, Craftsmanship
	Counselor	Mercy, Wisdom, Prophecy

Learning what the spiritual gifts are, what they are not, and how God intends them to function is crucial when it comes to identifying which gift or gifts God has given you. But it takes more than just reading about them. Prayer, reflection, experience, and meaningful feedback from people who know you well will provide the additional insights needed to identify and understand your spiritual gifts and to use them as you serve.

FOCUSED PRAYER

Lord,
thank you for giving me clarity around what spiritual gifts are—
and what they are not.
Help me grow in the fruit of your Spirit
by engaging in spiritual practices
that draw me closer to you
so I can better reflect your love
to those around me.
Help me develop habits that grow me
toward spiritual maturity.
From a foundation of Christlikeness,
help me maximize the impact of my spiritual gifts
through the one and only life
you have given me to live.
Amen.

REFLECTION:
Questions for Journaling or Discussion

1. Why do you think it's important to be clear about what the spiritual gifts are—and what they are not?
2. Which of the four things listed below is hardest for you to differentiate from a spiritual gift? Explain.
   Natural talents
   Fruit of the Spirit
   Spiritual practices
   Position titles
3. To further your own journey toward spiritual maturity, which spiritual practices are you curious to engage in more deeply?
4. Reflect on your current relational roles and organizational positions at work, in your church, or in the community. Based on how you understand your spiritual gifts, what may need to change? How can you make relational, ministry, and marketplace choices that are based more closely on your gifts?
5. What insight from this chapter gives you a better understanding of who you are—and gives you greater freedom to live as God made you to be?

WHERE IS IT WRITTEN?
Scripture Passages for Further Study

Therefore, whether you eat or drink, or whatever you do, do all things for the glory of God.   1 Corinthians 10.31

1 Corinthians 13.1–8
Galatians 5.22–23
James 1.16–18

Relational Style

7 YOU'VE GOT STYLE!

I want you to do a little experiment. When I tell you what to do, don't overthink it or analyze it; just do it. Ready? Here it is.

Set the book down and then cross your arms. Get comfortable. With your arms crossed, glance down and notice the position of your hands and arms.

Great! Now let your arms go and relax.

I'd like you to do it again, but this time reverse your arms by putting the opposite arm on top. Got it? Okay. Now give it a try.

Was it a little more challenging the second time? Uncomfortable? Did you have to think about it in order to get your arms to cooperate? While you *could* do it, my guess is it didn't feel natural. It took focus and felt a little awkward.

There is no right or wrong arm-crossing technique. Left-arm-over-right is just as "correct" as right-arm-over left. Both are acceptable; they are just different. The first time you crossed your arms, it was easy because you did it the way you've always done it. It didn't require much thought because it turns out you have your own natural way of crossing your arms.

The same is true of your relational style. Your God-given relational style is the way you prefer to relate to others and the world around you. It shows up in how you naturally func-

Your God-given relational style is the way you prefer to relate to others and the world around you.

tion and engage others in a social, work, or ministry setting. It's your most natural, God-given way of relating to others. Your relational style energizes you because it is what comes naturally to you. It's uniquely yours, and it leaves you feeling filled up.

God created us with natural preferences. Each of us is more comfortable relating in certain ways than we are in other ways.

Your relational style is the second critical part of your profile. It answers questions like:

> How can I best serve?
> What is the most life-giving way for me to engage others?
> What refuels me when I'm depleted?

As we interact in our various relationships, we can't always relate the way we prefer. There are certain people with whom we need to adjust our style in order to meaningfully connect with them. They may be doing the same to connect with us.

When we relate in ways outside our relational style, it isn't as comfortable and often requires additional time, energy, caution, and sensitivity. It's similar to crossing your arms the opposite way: you *can* do it, but it takes a little more effort. While we each have a preferred style of relating, most of us can relate in other ways at any given time.

While we each have a preferred style of relating, most of us can relate in other ways at any given time.

What if you could live your everyday life in ways that reflect your relational style? What if you could find opportunities, positions, and experiences that actually fit your relational style? You can be sure of one thing—you'd experience far more energy! Functioning outside of our relational style is draining. In this way, we operate much like a battery.

The purpose of a battery is to dispense energy. A battery can only give out energy until it is drained. Then it becomes useless until it is recharged.

For each of us, there are some things that give us energy and some things that take energy from us. And like a battery, when we get drained of energy, we need to be recharged.

But what if we could do more things that give us energy? What if some of our activities throughout the day charged us up? Sure, some things will take energy from us, but what if we could recharge our battery by tapping into our relational style?

STORY: Jake and Ariana

Every time Jake attends a meeting, he shows up early because he likes to chat and catch up with everyone as they arrive. If he can't arrive early enough to mingle with the team, he feels frustrated and disconnected. He finds it harder to focus on the meeting because he's still wanting to engage everyone personally. People give him energy.

Ariana comes to the office a little early each morning as well. She goes straight to her desk, logs on to her laptop, and sorts through her emails. She responds to each one with the information her teammates or customers need. As others arrive, she could stop to visit, but she rarely does. She is energized by getting people their information and completing tasks so others have what they need to start their day. Accomplishing tasks that help people gives her energy.

Starting his day in a cubicle with daily tasks would rob energy from Jake. It would drain his battery. And Ariana wouldn't want to sit around talking with people until after she had completed her tasks. Of course, both could function like the other, but neither would be comfortable. Over time, they'd grow discouraged. Their energy and joy levels would become depleted.

Some kinds of activities give us energy, and others drain our energy. We need to be energized in order to use our spiritual gifts and accomplish God's assignments for us in this world. God wired us to be energized in different ways. Let's take a look at what gives you energy— and what drains your energy.

HOW ARE YOU ENERGIZED?

Which energizes you more—interacting with people or accomplishing tasks that serve people? Which is more fulfilling? Both are meaningful and needed. Both must be done with excellence. But it's likely that one is more energy-giving to you than the other. Your God-given relational style pulls you toward one over the other.

People or Task?

God created some of us with a primary orientation toward people. We refuel our tanks by engaging with teammates, friends, and family. Relationships are our recharging source.

God created some of us with a primary orientation toward accomplishing tasks. We refuel our tanks by accomplishing tasks that serve people. Doing things that are needed and helpful is what gives us energy.

This doesn't mean that people-oriented individuals don't value the accomplishment of tasks. Nor does it mean that task-oriented people don't value relationships. These are two sides of a continuum that simply represent our ways of relating to the world around us.

Which gives you more energy—people or tasks? How you are energized indicates the first part of your relational style.

The second part is equally important.

HOW ARE YOU ORGANIZED?

When it comes to how we order our responsibilities and organize our goals and our lives, God has again created us with unique preferences. Some of us like the certainty of a structured schedule, while others prefer the freedom of a more spontaneous approach. As with people versus task, there is no right or wrong; each side of the continuum is just different.

Carlos and Ashley are making plans for a road trip from Chicago to Dallas. Carlos simply wants to pack a bag, throw it in the car, and head south. Ashley wants to go online, research the best routes, make hotel reservations, plan which historical markers to see, and choose which restaurants to hit along the way. Clearly they have very different ways of organizing their lives. Carlos is unstructured, while Ashley is structured.

Nisha has been asked to speak at a conference for a group of leaders on the topic "Impacting Women in Business." Two days before the event, her assistant asked her how she was planning to approach the subject. Her surprising response was, "I'm not sure. I'm taking several past talks with me. Once I get there, I'll read them through and decide which one to deliver. Or maybe I'll blend a couple of talks together."

Matthew, on the other hand, likes to have his life in order. When he knows something has to be done, he'd just as soon get it done now and not have to worry about it later. Every Sunday night, he plans out the coming week. He lines up all of his responsibilities and then prioritizes them—shopping, work, family time, errands, exercise, church activities, and community involvement. Unstructured Nisha likes giving herself options; structured Matthew likes planning his priorities.

How do you like to organize? Are you more structured or unstructured? Do you prefer to play it by ear or stick to a plan? Most of us can do both when necessary, but one way feels a lot more natural and comfortable to us. Do you know which way you are organized?

RELATIONAL STYLE PREFERENCES:
Where Are You on the Spectrum?

You may have been thinking you are not strictly a task person or a people person. Or perhaps you're not quite as casual as an unstructured person, but neither are you as committed to preplanning and organization as some structured people you know.

Relational style is a continuum. Few people would place themselves on the side of 100 percent "people" or 100 percent "task." Few would describe themselves as all "structured" or all "unstructured."

> **When we operate within our God-given relational style, our battery stays charged, we find greater joy in our daily activities, and we are better positioned to fulfill God's call on our lives.**

Most of us land somewhere along the continuum. We have a certain zone in which we are comfortable connecting with others, accomplishing our responsibilities, and functioning in life. When we consistently operate outside of that zone and move further away from our relational style, we will experience more boredom, stress, discontent, fatigue, or burnout. But when we operate within our God-given relational style, our battery stays charged, we find greater joy in our daily activities, and we are better positioned to fulfill God's call on our lives.

> **See directions to your online RIGHT4 YOU Profile on page 179.**

ASSESSMENT #2: Relational Style

Are you curious where you fall on the spectrum of People/Task and Structured/Unstructured? It's time to take your Relational Style Assessment.

If you don't have access to the RIGHT4 YOU Profile online, you can use the Relational Style assessment provided at the back of this book on page 193. Set aside about thirty minutes of uninterrupted time to complete Assessment #2: Relational Style.

Add your Relational Style to your RIGHT4 YOU Profile on page 180:

_____ + _____

(People or Task)   (Structured or Unstructured)

Your online results will look something like this:

YOUR PERSONAL STYLE

You appear to be a **People/Unstructured** person.

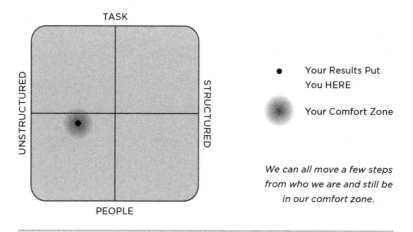

● Your Results Put You HERE

Your Comfort Zone

We can all move a few steps from who we are and still be in our comfort zone.

UNDERSTAND EACH QUADRANT

The results of your assessment will place you in one of four quadrants: People/Structured, People/Unstructured, Task/Structured, Task/Unstructured. Within each of those quadrants, there are variations. Those who are farther out toward the edge of their quadrant will tend to have stronger characteristics of that style than someone whose placement is closer to the center of the grid. Let's look at the characteristics that typically define each quadrant.

Continuum #1: Task or People
Task-Oriented
If you're more **task-oriented**, you likely exhibit these characteristics:

You are energized by...
- doing things that help people.
- accomplishing tasks.
- checking things off your to-do list.
- working with others who share your commitment to the task.
- completing a project that makes a difference.

You can feel drained, perturbed, or frustrated by an excess of relational, people-oriented activities.

People-Oriented
If you're more **people-oriented**, you likely exhibit these characteristics:

You are energized by...
- interpersonal relationships.
- tasks accomplished in groups.
- frequent interactions with people.
- projects that require face-to-face interactions.
- working with people in a team setting.

You can feel drained, awkward, or frustrated when juggling a bunch of tasks at once or when working in prolonged isolation.

Notice that both types of people value building relationships. Both value meeting goals. The difference is in *how* these things are accomplished.

Continuum #2: Unstructured or Structured

Unstructured

If you naturally prefer to function in a more **unstructured** style, you likely ...

- put everything into *piles.*
- are less concerned with being precise.
- prefer lots of options and flexibility.
- prefer a variety of activities.
- are comfortable in undefined situations.
- enjoy relationships that are spontaneous.

Structured

If you naturally prefer to function in a more **structured** style, you likely ...

- put everything into *files.*
- plan and bring order to your life—and others' lives.
- make decisions and seek closure.
- are more detail-oriented.
- like things clearly defined.
- enjoy stable, consistent relationships.

Both types of people value being organized. Both care about achieving excellence. The difference is in *how* they organize and *how* they achieve.

Now let's put the two continuums together and see how they create four quadrants.

UNDERSTANDING THE FOUR QUADRANTS

Task/Structured

If your relational style is **Task/Structured**, you tend to . . .

- get the job done.
- focus on results.
- seek measurable markers of success.
- follow directions and stick to the agenda.
- appreciate a boss or leader who provides clear expectations.

Task/Unstructured

If your relational style is **Task/Unstructured**, you tend to . . .

- appreciate general guidelines rather than specific directions.
- be versatile.
- help wherever needed.
- get tangible results using unconventional pathways.
- appreciate a boss or leader who sets expectations but gives freedom in how to achieve them.

People/Structured

If your relational style is **People/Structured**, you tend to . . .

- project warmth.
- like your relationships to be defined.
- relate well with others.
- appreciate a boss or leader who balances the team's culture with its effectiveness.
- enjoy tradition and familiar surroundings.

People/Unstructured

If your relational style is **People/Unstructured**, you tend to . . .

- be highly conversational.
- be flexible.
- relate well with others.
- appreciate a boss or leader who prioritizes the team's culture and its relationships.
- enjoy surprises and spontaneous situations.

Understanding your relational style will help you appreciate the way God designed you to interact with him and others to fulfill your you-shaped purpose in this world.

In the next chapter, we'll further explore how your style affects the way you hear, learn, and express your self.

FOCUSED PRAYER

Lord,
thank you for the colorful differences among us all
and for the ways we complement each other.
Thank you for the people lovers
and the task completers.
Thank you for the careful, precise organizers
and for those who sparkle with serendipity.
Hold up a mirror for me so I can see and accept my true self—
the person you created me to be.
Help me to be honest, direct, and respectful
with all the people you place in my life.
Help me to serve you and others
fearlessly and joyfully.
Amen.

REFLECTION:
Questions for Journaling or Discussion

1. Looking at your Relational Style results, what stands out most to you? Explain.
2. Can you think of a personal experience when the ways you prefer to be energized were not received well by those around you? Explain.
3. How has the way you organize your life caused tension in a personal or work relationship?
4. Can you think of a time when those around you stifled your relational style? How did it feel? How did you respond?
5. Knowing what you now know about your relational style, what will you do differently to both honor your style and create more harmony with those around you?
6. How can you and your team (those you serve or work alongside) better encourage and honor each other's relational styles?

WHERE IS IT WRITTEN?
Scripture Passage for Further Study

For you created my inmost being;
  you knit me together in my mother's womb.
I praise you because I am fearfully and wonderfully made;
  your works are wonderful,
  I know that full well.
My frame was not hidden from you
  when I was made in the secret place,
  when I was woven together in the depths of the earth.
Your eyes saw my unformed body;
  all the days ordained for me were written in your book
  before one of them came to be.

Psalm 139.13–16 NIV

DEVELOPING YOUR STYLE

8

YOUR RELATIONAL STYLE AND STYLE SHAPING

In the previous chapter, you identified your relational style—your preferences in regard to People/Tasks and Structured/Unstructured. Let's explore other factors that affect how we relate to others and function in our daily lives.

Growing up, we all experienced different expectations from people of influence in our lives. Parents, relatives, teachers, coaches, and other leaders may have taught us that acceptance is dependent on our willingness to relate in ways others expect.

Well-meaning (or sometimes not-so-well-meaning) people shaped your thinking about what's appropriate when it comes to how you relate to others and function in your daily life. Whether in intentional or unintentional, stated or unstated, healthy or dysfunctional ways, each of us learned to relate and behave in a manner that may not truly reflect our primary God-given relational style.

For example, imagine that both of your parents were structured and you were unstructured. Throughout your childhood and adolescence, you might have heard comments like:

"Why can't you keep your room clean?"
"You'd better get organized."
"How can you ever find anything in this mess of a desk?"

"You are such a procrastinator! Next time, plan ahead."
"Why do you always wait until the last minute?"

Or if both your parents were unstructured and you are structured, you might have heard things like:

"You are such a neat freak!"
"Can't you just have a little fun?"
"What's the hurry? You can finish that assignment next week."
"Don't remind *me* that it's time to go. I'm the grown-up here!"
"Just relax!"

In order to feel loved and accepted, we often try to conform to the style of those we are with to meet their expectations and gain their approval. The values in our family system and other significant relationships affect the way we interact and how we're perceived—by our self and others.

This kind of pressure to conform to someone else's style doesn't end in childhood. Conformity often follows us into adulthood, where we may feel we should relate in styles similar to those of our spouses, bosses, and other people we admire. If our relational style truly mirrors theirs, all is probably well. But if it is fundamentally different, we may feel tension, awkwardness, judgment, rejection, or even fear.

These types of influences can hinder your ability to receive the love and grace Christ extends to you. He made you to be fully free so you can be all that he created and called you to be. Without that freedom, you'll find that the development of your life's purpose will be hampered.

Remember, the God who designed you has not changed. You don't have to live in reaction to the opinions and expectations of others. Be comfortable and unapologetic about the person God made you to be. If reaching that level of freedom seems impossible, talk with a trusted friend, spiritual leader, or counselor. Jesus died to make us free!

Each of us is dysfunctional to some degree. It's part of living in a fallen and sinful world. The more dysfunction we experienced in our formative years, the more difficult it can be to work through these matters of identity and purpose.

Be encouraged. You are on a journey toward truth and freedom. When the truth is unclear, seek clarity. Take what you know to be true about who God says you are and turn it into confidence. Embrace every inch of the freedom you have in Christ.

HEARING GOD THROUGH YOUR RELATIONAL STYLE

When I became a Christian at the age of eighteen, I had never read the Bible and didn't know much about the life of Jesus. Someone told me to start reading the Gospels[1] in order to get to know Jesus better.

I read through the book of Matthew and wasn't too far into Mark's gospel when I realized many stories repeated themselves. Had Mark copied portions from Matthew? That seemed like plagiarism. As I continued into Luke, I found more repeated stories. I was confused. Why did God allow this to happen, especially in the Bible? I began to wonder why there were four gospels if so many stories were the same.

Does God stutter? Why did he need to repeat himself? Why are there four versions of the same story? Perhaps you've wondered the same thing.

It wasn't until later in my study of Scripture that I began to understand. Each gospel is written from a different historical and personal perspective to appeal to the different styles of four unique audiences.

God uses relational styles to tell his story:

The gospel of Matthew was written by someone who was likely people/structured in style, for an educated, Jewish-Christian audience.

The gospel of Mark was written by someone who was likely people/unstructured in style.

The gospel of Luke was written by a task/structured person who was a physician by trade.

The gospel of John was written by a people/unstructured person—someone who was a close friend of Jesus and who wrote other New Testament books with a heavy theme of loving others. John's relational and poetic style flows in a very different way from the style of Luke the physician.

Most of us approach our understanding of God through the eyes of our relational style. We read and relate to Scripture according to our style preferences.

People: If you are energized through people, you may have a tendency to place a higher value and emphasis on themes like love, forgiveness, fellowship, community, and grace.

Task: If you are task-oriented, you may focus more on such themes as sharing your faith, making disciples, praying, and avoiding evil. Obeying, committing, and serving are the concepts that likely energize you.

Structured: You may be prone to pick up on passages about judgment, law, order, preparation, and justice.

Unstructured: You likely gravitate toward walking by faith, being filled with the Spirit, not worrying, and trusting.

At least one of the four gospels will connect with your relational style. No matter how God has wired you, he has provided a means for you to personally relate to him and his Word so that you can better relate to others and the world.

> No matter how God has wired you, he has provided a means for you to personally relate to him and his Word so that you can better relate to others and the world.

No matter how you see God, you do not see all of him. None of us can. We need each other to complete our understanding of his fullness. Each of us needs what we lack in order for the body of Christ to be balanced and healthy.

And just as others can enhance your understanding of God, you can enhance theirs. Be the person God made you to be, confident that what you offer through your relational style is vital to the body of Christ—vital but incomplete. We need each other in community to experience more of who God is.

A WORD OF CAUTION

Identifying your relational style helps you understand why and how you do some of the things you do in your relationships. Your relational style may explain your behavior; it doesn't excuse it.

Just because you are an unstructured person doesn't mean it's okay for you to miss deadlines. And being a structured person doesn't excuse you from needing to be flexible at times.

Your relational style may explain your behavior; it doesn't excuse it.

A significant part of your design is revealed through your relational style. It's another way you can see God's divine fingerprints on your life. As a part of your RIGHT4 YOU Profile, your relational style indicates the unique way your spiritual gifts will be best expressed. It works within your life passion, which is where we're headed next.

FOCUSED PRAYER

Lord,
thank you for designing me with intention.
Each part of me is the result of your creative love.
Each part of me wants to be energized and organized
according to how you wired me.
I am grateful for the unique ways you give me
to relate to others and the world around me.
Thank you for how you so carefully made me
to be me!
I want to live without excuses.
Help me live on purpose—
and with purpose.
Help me to be an authentic and genuine follower of Christ.
Amen.

REFLECTION:
Questions for Journaling or Discussion

1. "Your relational style explains your behavior; it doesn't excuse it." Agree? Disagree? Explain.
2. How does your relational style affect the way you view and understand God? How does it affect the way you view and understand others?
3. Share one of your childhood messages that you now know is not true of you. What practical step can you take to live into who God made you to be?
4. From what you've learned about your relational style, what roles in your faith community, neighborhood, school, or work would best fit you and honor the way God designed you?

WHERE IS IT WRITTEN?
Scripture Passages for Further Study

Check out each of these followers of Christ in Scripture. From their words in the passages below, what can you learn about their personal styles?

Disciple	Scripture Passage
John	John 1.14; 3.16–17; 10.11–18; 11.35; 14.16–18; 1 John
Luke	Luke 1.1–4
Peter	John 18.10
Paul	1 Corinthians 9.19–23
Thomas	John 20.24–25

Life
Passion

9 WHAT'S THE BIG DEAL ABOUT PASSION?

Knowing how you've been formed by God informs you about *how* you can make a meaningful, you-shaped contribution in this world and enjoy a purposeful life. But *where* should you be making that contribution? To answer this question, let's explore the concept of passion.

WHAT I LEARNED ABOUT MY HEART

Traffic was heavy as I drove across town. I was mentally focused on an upcoming meeting when the light turned red and I stopped. Some movement near the curb caught my eye. I turned and saw a man in his forties dressed in tattered clothes. He was digging through a public trash can, pulling out aluminum cans and plastic bottles and putting them in his shopping cart. The cart also held bags of what I assumed were his earthly possessions. My thoughts turned from my meeting agenda to this obviously homeless man.

I wondered how he became homeless. How long had he been on the streets? Did he have a family? A wife? Children? Where were his friends? Did his parents know his situation? Did he struggle with a mental illness or addiction? Could he work? If so, why didn't he? What did he do during cold winter nights? Where did he sleep? Did anybody care?

I began to think about other homeless people I'd seen downtown. Images of children living on the streets and in cars flooded my thoughts. I felt sad and overwhelmed by the complexities of this societal challenge.

Then the signal turned green and I drove on.

I didn't do anything for that man. While I give time and money to several other causes, I don't do anything for those who are homeless. Do I lack compassion? Am I a bad person? Some people might say I am.

Have you seen people or situations that tug at your heart, but for some reason, you do nothing? Why?

The answer may be found in understanding the difference between compassion and passion.

WHAT IS PASSION?

When I use the term *passion* for the purposes of this book, I'm describing a God-given desire that compels us to make a difference in a particular area of life so that God is honored and people benefit.

> Passion is a God-given desire that compels us to make a difference in a particular area of life so that God is honored and people benefit.

When we respond to our God-given passions by using our spiritual gifts and relational style to make a difference, we find meaning, significance, and purpose.

IDENTIFY YOUR PASSION

Identifying your God-given passion is not an exact science; it's more of an art. It's a process that helps us find words to name the causes, people, or things we care about most deeply—things that are also close to the heart of our compassionate God.

Take a look at some types of passions below to see if any of them trigger a "yes!" in you.

Types of Passion

A passion for a people group, such as children, teens, or senior citizens. Passions can be more specific—like passion for those who are grieving, newly married, incarcerated, or blind. You may have a passion for mothers of preschoolers, those with special needs, those who are homeless, or single parents.

A passion for a cause, such as homelessness, world hunger, clean water, human rights injustice, the environment, animal rights, financial stewardship, governmental policies, or outreach to those who are spiritually lost, marginalized, or disenfranchised.

A passion for a role or function, such as mentoring people who are new to faith, being an entrepreneur, or consulting executives. You may find it fulfilling to serve as a coach, coordinator, researcher, or systems developer.

People who are drawn to a role or function often list several passion areas, but upon further exploration, they realize that in each of the areas on their list, they're functioning in similar ways. It's the role or function itself that ignites their passion, no matter what the cause may be.

Putting your passion into words gives you clarity. Clarity helps you narrow your focus on where you should invest your spiritual gifts, talents, and time, which helps you say no to things outside your passion area. Once you're clear about the people, cause, role, or function God has planted in your heart, you can move forward with confidence that you're fulfilling your life's purpose.

Two Signs That You've Identified Your Passion

One sign that you've identified your passion is that you feel frustrated that others are less committed to it than you. *What's wrong with people?* you may wonder. *Can't they see how important my area of passion is?*

Another sign is that you feel joy and excitement when you stumble across someone who shares your same passion. *This person gets it!* you think. Your conversation is invigorating, and often plans begin to form. This is how some of the most passionate teams of difference makers are born.

PURSUE YOUR HEART'S DESIRE

You can't do everything. You can't fix every broken system or right every wrong in this world. But are you doing something in the area of passion that God has put in your heart?

None of us can fix everything that needs fixing. None of us can care about every people group, cause, role, or function in this world. We can't, and so we don't. We just don't have that capacity.

God, on the other hand, cares about every need and has the capacity to perceive every wrong that should be righted in this world. So God placed a piece of his heart into your heart so you can join him in his kingdom purposes. Your passion is that piece of God's heart.

> *God placed a piece of his heart into your heart so you can join him in his kingdom purposes. Your passion is that piece of God's heart.*

By pursuing your passion, you respond to what God placed inside you to give your life direction, meaning, and purpose.

In the Old Testament, God gave the shepherd David a huge passion: to lead the nation of Israel, which he did when he became their king. David wrote these words in the book of Psalms:

> Trust in the LORD and do good;
>> dwell in the land and enjoy safe pasture.
> Take delight in the LORD,
>> and he will give you the desires of your heart.
>
> *Psalm 37.3–4 NIV*

A remarkable if/then proposition! What must God's people do? Trust, do good, dwell where God placed them, enjoy their lives there, and take delight in God. What does God do? Gives them the desires of their heart.

When I first read this passage, I took it at face value—that whatever my heart desired, God would be obliged to give it to me if I met the conditions. But the passage speaks of a cause-and-effect relationship.

When I live my life in the way described, God gives me my desires. I can then be passionate about those things God has given me to be passionate about.

Jesus teaches the same principle in the New Testament: "If you remain in me, and my words remain in you, ask whatever you wish, and it will be done for you."[1]

What do we do? "Remain" in Christ, and his words "remain" in us. The concept is we live and dwell in Christ. That's our part. And the result? What is God's part? Anything we wish will be done. *Anything?* Seriously? That's a significant promise.

Take a closer look. Many of us wish for many things—many good things that we think God would say yes to. When we remain in Christ, God's heart's desire for us becomes our heart's desire. We won't ask for something that doesn't seem to reflect God's desire. Therefore, we can ask confidently for what we desire, knowing that from our perspective, our requests reflect his purposes.

Sometimes our deepest wishes get a yes from God. But what about when we get a no? Those of us who are Christ followers and remain in him are being transformed by him, even in the no. Our will is learning to conform to his plan and his pacing. Over time and through much prayer, we learn to rest in God's goodness and faithfulness.

We have eternity on our side. Someday, the abiding yes will come.

A DEEPER LOOK AT PASSION

Let's explore how passion works in our lives.

Sam believes that students in middle school and high school are the most important age group to focus on when it comes to faith. "Students are developing their intellects and formulating impressions that will set the tone for the rest of their lives," he tells anyone who will listen. "Young people need to grow—not only emotionally, relationally, and intellectually, but *spiritually* as well!"

Sam is always trying to get others to do more for students.

He believes serving the needs of young people can solve so many of their problems and challenges in years to come.

Riya is committed to addressing issues of social injustice. It drives her crazy that the city council in her town views homelessness as an inconvenience for everyone else, all but ignoring the actual needs of the homeless population.

Can't they see how the policies got us here? she wonders. *We need to address the causes of homelessness, not just the symptoms.*

Riya spends her Saturdays working at a downtown homeless center and logs hours on her laptop. She tries to prompt policy changes by writing weekly to the city council, Congress, and state senators.

Desmond became a Christ follower in his thirties, and he remembers how it felt to be spiritually adrift throughout his college years and twenties. It makes sense, therefore, that he's passionate about talking to people who are curious about spiritual things and telling them his story. "What's more important than helping someone find their spiritual center in Christ?" he says.

Then there's Jenna, who's passionate about raising money to dig a borehole well in a tiny village in Kenya's bush country, where a lack of clean water is causing illness and death.

I could go on and on. Countless people groups, causes, and roles and functions all over the world are worthy of our time and best efforts. God cares about every single one of them. The fact that each of us cares about something different is part of God's design and in accordance with the assignment he has given us. God spreads out his passions among those he has called.

What about you? What do you care about most? Where would you like to have an impact? What issues burden you when you see and hear about them? When your mind wanders, what do you dream about? Has God given you a vision for how a wrong can be made right? Whatever term you use—*burden, dream, vision,* or *call*—your passion is the God-given desire of your heart to make a kingdom difference somewhere in this world.

God put a divine magnet within each of us that draws us to the people, causes, or roles and functions where he invites us to make a meaningful contribution. He has given you a passion that aligns with his purpose for your life.

THE PASSION OF THE APOSTLE PAUL

The apostle Paul was aware that his desire to preach to the Gentiles (unbelievers) was more than his own agenda; it was the fulfillment of a desire God had given him.[2] Before becoming a follower of Christ, Paul (also known as Saul) was a Jewish leader who showed his zeal for God by persecuting Christians. As Saul was traveling to the next town (Damascus), God showed up in the form of a light from heaven that flashed around Saul and asked, "Why do you persecute me?" Saul was temporarily blinded by the light and recognized the error of his ways.[3] He became an ardent Christ follower and gained clarity about where he was to focus and find his purpose.

It can be much the same with you, though perhaps without the drama of Saul's experience on the road to Damascus! A big part of understanding God's purpose for you is examining your own heart's desire—your passion.

MAKING A DIFFERENCE THROUGH YOUR PASSION

Thomas Edison is remembered for inventing the incandescent light bulb. Henry Ford is remembered for developing the assembly line mode of automobile production. The Reverend Dr. Martin Luther King is remembered for leading the Civil Rights Movement in the United States. What would you like to be remembered for?

Granted, most of us will never be as well-known as these people, but each of us has a life that matters. How will you spend your one and only life? What mark of personal significance do you want to leave behind? Even if your passion doesn't seem especially significant to others, it's the unique, distinct passion God gave to you. Pursue your passion!

TWO PASSION PITFALLS:
Passion Envy and Passion Projection

Once you have identified your passion, you are less likely to fall victim to fulfilling the passions of someone else. Nonetheless, each of us will be tempted at times to turn our focus from our unique passion to the passions of others.

Here are two passion pitfalls to avoid.

Passion Envy

If you are continuously saying yes to a role or cause that you know is outside your passion area because you envy others who serve or work in this area, you're robbing others of their responsibility to fulfill the passion God gave to *them*. Passion envy is no fun for either of you. Keep focused on *your* passion.

Passion Projection

We all know people who are so enthusiastic about their passion area that they expect everyone else to care about it as much as they do. Whether verbally or nonverbally, unspoken, intentionally or unintentionally, they project their passion onto us.

Don't let the passion projection of others distract you from your God-given assignment—and be careful not to project your passion onto others.

Whenever you encounter passion projection, simply applaud the other person's passion but continue to pursue your own. Don't let the passion projection of others distract you from *your* God-given assignment—and be careful not to project your passion onto others.

PASSION FOR A LIFETIME

Perhaps at this point, you don't have a clue what your God-given passion is. Or maybe you do know but don't know what to do about it. You may have shared it with a friend, spouse, parent, or coworker, only to have them respond with statements of skepticism or bewilderment, such as:

"Why on earth would you want to do that?"

"You're not smart enough" (or "spiritual enough" or "old enough").

"But you're a woman!" (or "a person of color" or some other historically suppressed person).

"That would be irresponsible." ("You have a mortgage, school loans, and so forth.")

"But how will you fund it?"

"That's great, but would your [parents, children, pastor, spouse, etc.] approve?"

If you've heard responses like these, you may have simply offered a nervous smile, nodded in polite agreement, and let the words of others push your passion back into the depth of your heart. I have good news. *Your passion was given to you by God—and it's a beautiful part of how you were designed.* God will not take it away. The apostle Paul reminds us of this truth: "God's gifts and his call are irrevocable."[4]

Just as a beach ball pushed under the water will keep popping up to the surface, so it is with your passion. Others can suppress it, but they can't make it go away. It *will* keep popping up. They can silence you, but they can't keep your passion from speaking out.

It takes effort to keep a beach ball underwater. How much energy do you plan to spend on keeping your passion submerged? A few months? A few years? The rest of your life? It's time to redirect your energy toward fulling your passion.

ALAN'S STORY: A Passion That Would Not Die

Some years ago, a friend told me a story about his father, Alan.

When Alan was in his early twenties, he had a strong desire to be a missionary pilot. Missionary pilots fly small planes into remote areas of the world, bringing supplies, staff, and equipment to local outposts, churches, and villages.

The training for this particular career is rigorous. Not only do you have to be a highly skilled pilot, but you also must be a master mechanic, able to repair engines with minimal access to parts and tools. It takes years of dedication and training to qualify.

Alan had that kind of diligence. After years of training and hundreds of hours in the air, the day finally came when he received his commercial pilot's certificate with the required instrument rating, along with his mechanic's certification.

He then located a mission agency and applied for the position that would bring together his two greatest passions—mission work and flying. For some reason, he did not get accepted. He wasn't sure why and didn't pursue it further.

For the next twenty years, Alan worked as a janitor at a local high school. It was an honorable job; however, it didn't fulfill his passion. His dream of becoming a missionary pilot had been suppressed.

"To this day," Alan's son told me, "whenever my dad is around planes or is involved with mission projects at his church, he lights up. He's a different person, filled with energy and enthusiasm."

Missions and flying remain his passion. Disappointment, rejection, and the suppression of his passion in his job did not change Alan's dual loves: flying and missions. Despite the barriers that kept him from turning his passion into a job, Alan caught glimpses of his passion as a layperson who volunteered for mission causes.

Whatever disappointment, rejection, or suppression you've experienced in pursuing your passion, know this: those things cannot defeat God's call.

With this understanding of what a passion is and the knowledge that God has placed a passion in you, let's get a better grasp of the you-shaped passion God has given you.

FOCUSED PRAYER

Lord,
thank you for placing your desires in my heart.
Help me see clearly and understand which
people groups, causes, roles, or functions
matter most to me.
I long to fulfill your call through the life passion
you've ignited in me.
Keep me from being unduly influenced
by those who may question my call
or hinder me from following you.
Keep me from stepping into the passions of others
or mistaking their passion for mine.
Help me stop, be still, and listen for your guidance.
Help me discover the why, where, when, and how
of your design and desire for my life—
and help me to follow my heart's desire.
In Jesus' name.
Amen.

REFLECTION:
Questions for Journaling or Discussion

1. When you read about the author's experience of seeing the homeless man at the red light (page 93), did it remind you of a time you saw a need and did not respond? Describe.
2. Have you ever been swept up in someone else's "passion projection" and turned your focus from your own passion to theirs? How can you better applaud their passion and pursue your own? Explain.
3. With all the legitimate and critical needs in the world, what can you do to retain a caring heart without feeling overwhelmed?
4. How does it make you feel to know that God desires to guide you toward addressing the needs he has specifically purposed for you?
5. When Alan's dreams of becoming a missionary pilot were thwarted (page 101), he continued to be involved in aviation and missions as a volunteer. Do you think it makes a difference to God whether you are a paid or unpaid server? Why?
6. What are your two most nagging questions right now about finding your life passion?

WHERE IS IT WRITTEN?
Scripture Passages for Further Study

"If you remain in Me, and My words remain in you, ask whatever you wish, and it will be done for you." Jesus, John 15.7

Psalm 37.3–5

Acts 9.1–31

Galatians 1.15–16

YOU'VE GOT PASSION!

Spiritual gifts are fairly defined, specific, and concrete. Relational styles have different variations within four basic quadrants. But the third characteristic in your RIGHT4 YOU Profile, life passion, is much more open-ended, addressing every conceivable area of human need. Passion is a matter of the heart, and because it's about our feelings, emotions, and desires, each of us may describe our passion with different words. You and I may be passionate about the same thing yet describe our passions quite differently.

Clarity is key when it comes to gaining focus among the vast array of passion areas available to us. And because clarity matters, words matter. In this chapter, we'll explore seven passion indicators to help you find the words that best describe your passion. Coming up with a word or a short, concise phrase that captures your heart's desires will better motivate you. And you'll come to see that you want to do something about it.

SEVEN PASSION INDICATORS

Before you take your passion assessment at the end of this chapter, let's look at the following passion indicators. Consider how some of these indicators can be windows into your heart and into what most moves you, and write your answers in the spaces below.

1. Passion Has Body Language

Imagine you and I meet for the first time. In the course of our conversation, we talk about a variety of things. When we hit on a certain topic, you start speaking a little faster and lean in as you speak. Your eyes light up, your body shifts, and maybe you begin to talk with your hands. Your voice gets a little higher and you become more animated. Your facial expressions become more dramatic.

In this scenario, what topics might you be talking about that would show up in your body language and emotional energy?

---

2. Passion Imagines

When we think about our area of passion, we often begin dreaming—both daydreams and actual dreams at night. Dreams allow your subconscious thoughts to explore a desire of your heart. You may visualize yourself being drawn in, as if by a current, in a way that enlarges your vision for the good you could do.

The images in your dreams often strike an emotional chord deep within you and spark a feeling of love, fear, sadness, or anger. You might get clarity around what you "ought" to do. You might imagine how you could make a difference for good—and be emotionally moved to do so.

When you ask yourself, *What if I . . . ?*, what is it that you imagine yourself doing? The answer may provide clarity about your passion.

---

3. Passion Brings Joy and Success

We can do things that give us great joy and also things that bring us success. Ask yourself, *Where do I experience both joy and success simultaneously?*

Your achievements or success may be things that others don't find particularly impressive, but they're important to you. Or you may have achieved something others find impressive—Student of the Year or Salesperson of the Quarter—but it wasn't that big of a deal to you, and the process of earning it didn't necessarily give you joy.

Perhaps when you were twelve, you and a friend decided to put on a neighborhood carnival. You organized the booths, found people to run them, collected prizes, made and sold tickets, and even made a little profit. You pulled it off and had a great time doing it. It brought you joy, and it was a success. No one handed you a major award for your efforts, but you were deeply satisfied and knew you had done well.

Or perhaps you volunteered to be a reading buddy for a child who had dyslexia, and you helped that child read her first book, cover to cover. No one really noticed your contribution—and certainly no one gave you a plaque for it—you felt deep joy seeing that child's sense of pride as she closed the last page of the book and reached for another. You knew you had achieved something worthwhile. You experienced joy plus success!

Think back on some of the most memorable moments of success in your life, both as a child or teen and in your adult years. Which of those achievements gave you great joy? List three to five of your joyful successes:

- _____
- _____
- _____
- _____
- _____

Now look at them again and note whether there are any similarities, parallels, or relationships in your list. Do you see any common themes, patterns, roles, or goals? What do you observe?

_____
_____
_____

4. Passion Absorbs

When you are in touch with your passion and operating within it, time can either stand still or fly by. As you become absorbed in your passion area, you may become less aware of what's going on around you.

Perhaps you get so focused on the one thing you care so much about that you fail to keep perspective on other things.

Has a friend, coworker, or partner ever commented on how you got so immersed in an activity that they couldn't get your attention? This type of intense engagement enables you to focus on meeting a need in a God-given passion area.

When you discover that three hours have passed and it felt like a mere thirty minutes, what kinds of things were you likely to have been doing?

_____

_____

_____

5. Passion Fulfills

When you're making a purposeful difference in an area of your passion, you'll feel a sense of satisfaction. The process may not always be easy or fun, but in the midst of it, you experience an inner confidence that you're doing what God wants you to do in the way he wants you to do it.

Has someone ever told you, "You were made for this!" Doing what you were made to do brings a sense of fulfillment. It just feels right.

Consider your current involvements. Where are you feeling most fulfilled? If you're not currently feeling fulfilled, where do you imagine you could be?

_____

_____

_____

6. Passion Energizes

Your passion motivates and energizes you. Not only do you become more alive emotionally when pursuing your passions; you actually gain more energy than you expend. This is God's way of moving you toward the people, causes, roles, or functions that are part of his agenda for your life. The energy you feel when you're operating in your sweet spot becomes your ongoing internal motivation.

What most energizes you?

_____

_____

_____

7. Passion Honors, Benefits, and Transforms

Your passion, when properly pursued, will pass a threefold test:

1. Does it honor God?
2. Does it benefit others?
3. Does it transform a community?

If your current pursuits—whether in your vocation or as a volunteer—don't accomplish these three things, they're probably not in your God-given areas of passion. They might be good things, but they may not be the best thing God has planned for you.

Of the passions you've considered thus far, which ones pass the test of honoring God, benefiting others, and transforming a community?

Response: _____

See directions to your online RIGHT4 YOU Profile on page 179.

ASSESSMENT #3: Life Passion

With the seven passion indicators in mind, let's turn now to your passion assessment. As you take your assessment, don't worry about when, where, or how you might pursue or fulfill your passion. Just focus on *what* your passion is. Try to put words to it. Name it.

Now take Assessment #3: Life Passion (about 30 minutes). Access your online assessment and enter your username and password (see page 179 for further details). After you've completed the assessment, click "RIGHT4 YOU Profile Results" to download a PDF file and print out your results.

Your online results will look something like this:

YOUR MINISTRY PASSION
You appear to have a passion to or for . . .

Teens and families in and outside the church. Raising leaders to meet these needs.

You feel your passion is in the area of . . .

First choice: **Equipping Ministries**
The heart of these ministries is maturing believers in the area of their gifts, ministry, training, and leadership. It serves a variety of life-stage and affinity groups for growth, accountability, and service.

Second choice: **Celebration Ministries**
The heart of these ministries is directed toward God by engaging the church in the Word, worship, song, the arts, and so forth.

If you don't have access to the online assessment, you can use the one provided at the back of this book on page 199.

Now you can get a holistic snapshot of your unique, God-designed self: Spiritual Gifts, Relational Style, and Life Passion.[1] Be sure to transfer your top results to complete a summary of your RIGHT4 YOU Profile on page 180.

PASSION CONFUSION

If you're still feeling a little unclear or uncertain about what your true passion is, consider three factors that can make it more challenging to understand your passion and give voice to it.

Passion Confuser #1: Outside Influences

Sometimes the values of those around us are so strong and dominant that to disagree with them is risky. You may fear rejection or a lack of approval if your passions are different from theirs.

Growing up in a variety of contexts—home, school, work, community, church—you may have felt differently from those who were in positions of authority. Because you trusted them, you adopted what they valued, which may have meant abandoning your own interests or passions.

As adults, we still have a strong need to belong. It's how God wired us—and that's a good thing. If you sense that pursuing your passion will put your sense of belonging at risk, it's tempting to submerge your passion and embrace the more "acceptable" passions of those around you.

If you could set aside the expectations of others for a moment and give yourself full permission to pursue your passion without judgment from family, friends, or people of influence, what passion would you pursue?

Jesus created and called you to be free to follow him. Your God-given passion won't go away, so surround yourself with supportive, understanding people who won't judge you because your passions differ from theirs. Find a community that will accept you unconditionally and encourage you to pursue your passion wholeheartedly.

Passion Confuser #2: People-Pleasing

Those who have a strong orientation toward pleasing others have a more difficult time identifying their own passions. Whether one's motivation for pleasing is intentional, subconscious, or a developed codependence, the result is the same.

If you tend to be a pleaser, it may feel wrong, illegal, or even selfish to say no to others. You're particularly at risk of passion projection. And once you've invested yourself in passions other than your own, it's harder to turn your focus to the passion God gave you.

Pleasers find it difficult to say, "I want to . . ." They're more comfortable accommodating others. If it makes you uneasy to declare your passion, try this exercise: Close your eyes and envision your audience of One—the God who lovingly created you and is excited to see you pursue the passion he gave you. With God at the forefront of your thoughts, finish this sentence: "I can't wait to get started doing this . . .

_____."

Passion Confuser #3: Multiple Passions

Some people find it easy to narrow their passion list down to three, four, or five passions, but then they get stuck. They can't focus in on their one or two true passion areas.

If this describes you, look at your list of three to five passion areas and try to find a theme or pattern among the areas you listed. Spend some time in prayer and reflection to discern the core themes of your passions.

Sometimes we're unable to see a central theme in our passions because of the various ways we're currently expressing it. If you can't spot specific passions or even a general area of passion, consider meeting with a trusted friend to help you find a word or brief phrase that captures the essence or theme of your passion. Often an outside perspective can help you see a bigger picture.

ANSWER THE WHERE QUESTION

Naming your passion answers the "where" question: "Where should I serve?" It directs you to where you should use your spiritual gifts and invest your time. To some degree, your answer to the where question isn't rocket science. It should be intuitive once you understand your gifts and passion.

If you have a passion for helping children, where should you be serving? *In a ministry or organization that is committed to impacting the lives of children.*

If your passion is for discipleship (helping people grow spiritually), where should you be serving? *On a team that is committed to discipling and equipping people to follow Christ.*

If your passion is for alleviating world hunger, where should you be serving? *In an organization committed to developing supply chains to better feed those who live in poverty.*

How about you? Without overthinking your response, complete the sentences below:

My passion is _____,
so I should be serving on a team committed to _____.

God has given you a passion. He has written it on your heart. Hopefully by now, it's clear to you where he is calling you to make a difference in this world. Your passion reveals the direction and heartfelt focus of your life's purpose.

Don't worry at this time how you can fulfill your passion. Perhaps you don't know of a team, church, or organization currently doing the work you'd love to do. Don't let that keep you from identifying your passion and asking God to help you fulfill it.

In the remaining chapters, you'll see how the integration and intersection of your God-given spiritual gifts, relational style, and life passion can lead to living a holistic life—one that is faithful, fruitful, and fulfilled.

FOCUSED PRAYER

Lord,
thank you for the passion you've given me.
As I look over my life, I'm amazed at all the indicators
you have given to make my life passion known.
Sometimes I struggle to stay focused
on the things that matter most to me.
Sometimes I get unduly influenced
or confused by those around me,
and I mistake their passions for mine.
Sometimes I long to fulfill my passion,
but I don't know where to begin.
Help me listen to my own heart
and not the expectations or judgments of others.
Guide me to the teams, ministries, or organizations
where I can most fulfill my calling.
Help me seek to please you—and you alone.
Amen.

REFLECTION:
Questions for Journaling or Discussion

1. Which of the seven passion indicators (pages 105–9) regularly show up in your own life? What do they tell you about your area(s) of passion?
   ○ has body language
   ○ imagines
   ○ brings joy and success
   ○ absorbs
   ○ fulfills
   ○ energizes
   ○ honors, benefits, and transforms
2. Which of these passion indicators would others most likely see in the way you express your passion?
3. Bruce identified three passion confusers (pages 111–12) that can make it difficult to identify your passion. What other things hinder you from gaining or maintaining passion clarity?
4. Imagine a day in the future when you're deeply involved in your passion area. You're pursuing it wholeheartedly and seeing the fruit of your efforts. What emotions do you feel as you imagine that day? What barriers do you foresee when it comes to making that day a reality?
5. Imagine a team or faith community where every person is using their spiritual gifts within their God-given area of passion. What would it feel like to be part of that community? How might those outside the community perceive its people?

WHERE IS IT WRITTEN?
Scripture Passages for Further Study

"These things I have spoken to you so that My joy may be in you, and that your joy may be made full."   Jesus, John 15.11

Isaiah 25.1   Romans 15.13

Romans 12.2   Other: _____

THE

DEVELOPING

YOU

PUTTING THE PIECES TOGETHER

It was one of those evenings—cold, windy, and rainy. My family and I were housebound—and bored. No one felt like playing a board game. There was nothing worth watching on television, and nothing to stream that we could all agree on. Out of desperation, we decided to do a jigsaw puzzle.

Digging through the closet, we found an unopened puzzle at the back of the top shelf—a Christmas present from several years earlier that had never been touched.

The puzzle had one thousand pieces. Clearly it would require more time, energy, and patience than the sixteen-piece animal puzzle I often helped my four-year-old daughter put together.

But it was the perfect activity for just such a night. In fact, it would capture our best energies for more than one night. We made a pact not to give up until the puzzle was finished, and with that, out came the card table.

We broke the seal and opened the box. Inside were a thousand tiny pieces, each holding a little piece of the big picture on the front of the box. We gathered around as we dumped all the pieces onto the card table. Our first task was to turn all the pieces so their colored sides faced up. It wasn't difficult and didn't take long, but it was a necessary first step.

As we flipped all the pieces, we separated out any pieces with straight edges that would form the outer border of the puzzle and put them in a pile. We especially kept our eyes peeled for pieces with two straight edges—the corners! Those four pieces would be the anchors of the whole border.

Not being a master at solving puzzles, I placed the top of the box on the edge of the card table so we could see what our finished product was supposed to look like. It was a beautiful nature scene with blue skies, green pastures, and a barn. We took the corner pieces and started connecting the edges. At this point, we were being guided more by the colors and their placement according to the box than by the actual shapes themselves.

We put the sky pieces on the top edges of the frame and the green grass pieces along the bottom. The sides held a combination of pieces— grass, barn, and sky. Once the border was done, it was simply a matter of filling it in with the remaining pieces.

It took two more days to get the right pieces in place to complete the puzzle. Once we finished, we stepped back and marveled at the beautiful colors and shapes of the pieces—and how they all fit together perfectly. We felt a sense of accomplishment.

No single piece represented the full picture, but each piece played a vital part. Only when all the pieces were properly connected did the whole picture become clear.

IT TAKES MORE THAN HAVING ALL THE PIECES

Common sense tells us that shaking a box that contains all the puzzle pieces and pouring them out onto a table will not produce a completed picture. We can be committed. We can be persistent. We can know we have all the right pieces of our profile in a box, but only the process of properly putting those pieces together will lead to seeing a complete picture of God's purpose for us.

Through your RIGHT4 YOU Profile, you have been introduced to the three core elements of how God designed you, and each is a vital piece of the picture God has for your life. Perhaps some of the things in your profile aren't new to you; they are pieces you have known or suspected were part of your picture, in one form or another. Others, perhaps, were a surprise. Either way, now you have your pieces.

So let's put your pieces on the table and see how they fit together to get a better picture of what God sees for you.

RIGHT4 YOU PROFILE: Spiritual Gifts + Relational Style + Passion

You've spent time learning, evaluating, and discussing three aspects of how God designed you: your spiritual gifts, relational style, and life passion. These three make up your RIGHT4 YOU Profile. Let's now take a moment to review and summarize your profile below (see page 180 if necessary).

My RIGHT4 YOU Profile

Spiritual Gift(s)	1. 2. 3.
Relational Style	_____ + _____ (Task or People) (Structured or Unstructured)
Passion	

These are your puzzle pieces. It's time to fit them together.

CONNECTING YOUR PASSION AND GIFTS

The relationship between your passion and your gifts is powerful. Your gifts are your God-given abilities, whereas your passion identifies where you want to make a difference. You can have any passion with any spiritual gift.

You can have any passion with any spiritual gift.

Passion helps you connect with others who share your interests. People with like-minded passions experience a bond and a common commitment. They often see the world in similar ways in the areas that matter most to them. Examples:

Passion	Gifts	Possible Expressions
Children	Administration	Plan agenda, crafts, activities, or check-in/check-out procedures
		Strategically plan lessons, events, goals
		Organize people and resources to impact kids
	Teaching	Write curriculum
		Teach a class or small group; tutor students
		Teach parenting skills for healthy child development
	Mercy	Work with struggling kids and their families
		Alleviate sources of dysfunction/pain in kids
		Advocate for children who have special needs
Discipleship (growing spiritually)	Hospitality	Create safe places and times for spiritual conversations
		Connect new people so everyone is valued and feels a sense of belonging
		Invite spiritual mentors to your gatherings
	Encouragement	Come alongside others as they explore faith
		Challenge people who are spiritually complacent
		Point people to trust in the promises of God
	Intercession	Ask God's Spirit to reveal truth for deeper faith
		Listen for God's voice in making decisions
		Pray for others to understand God's grace

Notice that passion is the umbrella under which your gifts will be most fruitful. Beneath the framework of this umbrella, you can then deploy your gifts and begin to imagine simple and creative ways to make a contribution to something you really care about.

Spiritual gifts are specific expressions, whereas passions can have a broader focus. To avoid confusing your passions with your spiritual gifts, use clear language. Avoid describing your passion with words or phrases commonly used to describe spiritual gifts.

Passion Words	Gift Words
reach people who are far from God	evangelism, prophecy, apostleship
steward finances	giving, faith, leadership, encouragement
equip God's people	teaching, wisdom, creative communication
connect those who are unconnected	hospitality, shepherding, administration

Clear language eliminates potential confusion and frees you to better understand where you desire to contribute versus what you're gifted to do.

CONNECTING YOUR GIFTS AND STYLE

Just as your passions and spiritual gifts share a powerful connection, your spiritual gifts and relational style connect powerfully as well. And just as you can have any passion with any spiritual gift, you can have any spiritual gift with any relational style.

You can have any spiritual gift with any relational style.

We tend to stereotype a spiritual gift with a relational style. For example, if someone has the gift of evangelism, they must be people-oriented, outgoing, and somewhat bold, right? Wouldn't it take that kind of relational style to talk with another person about faith? Or if someone has the gift of administration, we think they must be a task-oriented person who craves structure.

Stereotyping keeps us from seeing the variety of ways God intends gifts to be expressed through all kinds of relational styles. It inhibits people from leaning into their gifts because they don't fit the stereotype. It can make them doubt if they even have a particular gift at all.

Remember, gifts are what you *do* and your relational style is *how* God wired your preferred way of relating while using your gifts. Examples:

Spiritual Gift	Relational Style	Possible Expressions
Leadership	Task / Structured	1. Give direction and oversee the plan. 2. Assign roles and provide specific next steps. 3. Create short- and long-term goals to fulfill the mission.
	Task / Unstructured	1. Provide hands-on help to discern the best path forward. 2. Observe what others have done and then take the next step. 3. Give clear directions and delegate others to develop an effective process.
	People / Structured	1. Make good use of people's differences to best accomplish the mission. 2. Interact with each team member to pursue team synergy. 3. Organize the mission around relational energy in the group.
	People / Unstructured	1. Build a healthy team culture with subordinates who will carry out the vision. 2. Delegate the specifics to others who are detail-minded. 3. Encourage managers to use their gifts to the fullest.

Spiritual Gift	Relational Style	Possible Expressions
Creative Communication	Task / Structured	1. Design or create sets, lighting schematics, or choreography for a live event. 2. Build a spreadsheet that helps ensure deliverables happen and the message moves forward on schedule. 3. Write a month's worth of compelling social media posts.
	Task / Unstructured	1. Focus on a clear message. 2. Incorporate different elements to enhance the message. 3. Arrange the flow with a variety of sights, sounds, emotions.
	People / Structured	1. Write daily tweets that capture your organization's personality. 2. Choreograph the dance team's next performance. 3. Brainstorm themes for this year's Christmas party.
	People / Unstructured	1. Interview guests on a casual, fun podcast that tells people's stories. 2. Write human interest blogs that communicate the why behind your organization's mission. 3. Deliver talks or messages that engage people's emotions.

SAME GIFT, DIFFERENT STYLES: Ling and Kurt

Here's an example of the different ways our spiritual gifts can be expressed, depending on our relational styles.

Ling has a task-structured relational style. With her gift of mercy, she serves as an advocate for those who need financial assistance. Kurt also has the gift of mercy, but his people-unstructured style works best in the role of counselor for those in crisis or emotional distress.

While both have the same spiritual gift, Ling serves better on an organizational level, and Kurt serves better on the personal or relational level. Both are powerful forces in their respective areas, effectively using the gift of mercy to benefit those who are in need.

FRUITFUL BUT UNFULFILLED: Jazmin

For almost two years, Jazmin was involved with a community-based program as part of a building crew that constructs or refurbishes apartments for families who are homeless. She was good at her work, and her manager was pleased. However, Jazmin felt increasingly unfulfilled. To understand why, let's take a look at her profile.

RIGHT4 YOU Profile: Jazmin

Spiritual Gift(s)	Relational Style	Passion
Encouragement, Mercy	People/Structured	Help the homeless

Jazmin developed warm relationships with her crewmates because they shared a common passion—namely, providing housing for homeless families. Although she saw the fruit of her team's efforts, she didn't sense the feeling of affirmation or fulfillment she expected. After some reflection and conversations with a few wise friends, she understood why.

Jazmin had joined the team because she had an emotional desire (passion) to make a difference for families who are homeless. But her gifts of encouragement and mercy were not being utilized. Being on the work crew met her passion area (homelessness) and her love of structure, but it didn't capture the full expression of her gifts. She wanted to encourage the families they served and build relationships with them directly. She wanted to hear their stories personally and equip them to break free from poverty. No wonder she felt unfulfilled.

She spoke with her manager, who offered her a chance to be trained as a case worker. Jazmin jumped at the chance. She got the necessary certifications and began working with families directly, helping them navigate social services and offering them encouragement as they took steps toward independent living.

In this new role within the organization, Jazmin used her gifts in a way that allowed her people-oriented style to flourish. As she developed relationships with her clients, she watched them become more independent under her guidance and encouragement. Jazmin moved from rebuilding homes to rebuilding lives—and she found real fulfillment at last.

BRAINSTORMING THE POSSIBILITIES: Lucas

Lucas is new to the concept of spiritual gifts, relational styles, and passion, but he's eager to find a place where he can use all his God-given puzzle pieces to make a difference in this world. Here's his profile.

RIGHT4 YOU Profile: Lucas

Spiritual Gift(s)	Relational Style	Passion
Encouragement, Giving, Teaching	People/Structured	Steward finances

After completing his online assessments, he's been brainstorming possible roles. Here's what he has come up with so far:

- seminar instructor for retirement planning
- budget counselor
- writer of a training process for creating a family budget
- member of his church's budget committee
- benevolence board member
- fundraiser for a community nonprofit

How did he do? Can you see how each of these potential roles might be fulfilling for him? What might you add to Lucas's list? What possible snags do you see?

THE SKY'S THE LIMIT: You!

Before we get a little more personal and practical regarding potential roles to fit your profile, a word of caution. Don't limit your thinking. Dream limitless possibilities.

It's time for blue-sky thinking. You're not trying to squeeze yourself into someone else's version of your potential. You're not even trying to place yourself into a role, team, or organization that currently exists. You're simply imagining what it would look like and feel like to express your full RIGHT4 YOU Profile—your gifts and relational style and passion, *all at the same time*!

Too often we fill our days functioning in one role that utilizes our gifts, another that fits our style, and still another that pursues our passion. Imagine if you could find one role that allowed you to embrace *all* of who God made you to be. The simplicity, focus, and joy this would bring to your life—let alone the number of hours you would save—make it well worth pursuing such a dream. And those in your life will benefit too.

If money, time, education, or relationships were not a barrier, what could you do best?

The sky's the limit! If money, time, education, or relationships were not a barrier, what could you do best?

Assume such a position could exist. Innovate. Dream up a few roles where you can bring all of yourself to the table and fully be the you God created you to be.

Based on your RIGHT4 YOU Profile (page 179), brainstorm some specific role possibilities for your self. Write down every opportunity you can imagine (use extra paper if needed).

Blue-sky roles or opportunities:

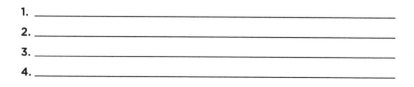

1. _____

2. _____

3. _____

4. _____

5. _____

6. _____

7. _____

God knows the purpose for which he created and called you, and he wants you to know too! It is God's intention for you to be faithful, fruitful, and fulfilled in him.

Jesus said,

> "Remain in me, as I also remain in you. No branch can bear fruit by itself; it must remain in the vine. Neither can you bear fruit unless you remain in me.
>
> "I am the vine; you are the branches. If you remain in me and I in you, you will bear much fruit ... This is to my Father's glory, that you bear much fruit, showing yourselves to be my disciples.
>
> "As the Father has loved me, so have I loved you. Now remain in my love ... I have told you this so that my joy may be in you and that your joy may be complete."   *John 15.4–5, 8–9, 11 NIV*

Are you starting to get the picture of the you God created you to be? This picture will give you freedom. It's your calling. It's your purpose in life, and your best efforts will benefit others, transform communities, and honor God.

FOCUSED PRAYER

Lord,
I'm beginning to understand why I enjoy some things
and find others so frustrating.
Help me stretch my imagination to find the areas of service
that best suit the profile of who you made me to be.
Lead me to the right people,
open the right doors,
and provide me with the right insights and opportunities
to be fruitful, fulfilled, and at peace
in the center of your design for my life.
Help me put together the puzzle pieces
so I can see.
Amen.

REFLECTION:
Questions for Journaling or Discussion

1. As you put together the puzzle pieces of your RIGHT4 YOU Profile (page 180), what jumps out at you that you've never noticed before? Explain.

2. Most people need time to consider how the parts of their profile work together. But right now, what is your biggest question?

3. Describe a time when you confused your spiritual gifts, relational style, and life passion. How might that situation have turned out differently if you'd had more clarity?

4. Consider the concept, "You can have any spiritual gift with any personal style and with any life passion," which we explored in this chapter. What personal significance does this reality have for you? Explain.

5. Of the possible roles you listed on pages 128–29, which two or three excite you the most? Which would be most challenging? Which would bring you the greatest fruitfulness and fulfillment?

6. How would your family, vocation, and faith community be different if everyone were living and serving according to their profile?

WHERE IS IT WRITTEN?
Scripture Passages for Further Study

And we know that God causes all things to work together for good to those who love God, to those who are called according to His purpose.   Romans 8.28

Matthew 6.10   Ephesians 4.15–16

1 Corinthians 3.5–9   Philippians 4.6–7

12 TIMING, AVAILABILITY, MATURITY, DEVELOPMENT

Choosing to invest your spiritual gifts, relational style, and passion in meaningful and significant activities is a wise choice you won't regret. Now that you've brainstormed some expressions of involvement you could pursue that fit your RIGHT4 YOU Profile, it's time to take stock of how you incorporate new activities into your already busy life—and perhaps eliminate some old, outdated ones.

Whether this means doing more, getting redirected within existing activities, or approaching the right activities differently, slow down long enough to make meaningful changes. You have the power to say yes to the right types of activities and the freedom to say no to other pursuits. Some of those pursuits may have been good, but as business author Jim Collins has put it, "Good is the enemy of great."[1] And you were meant for greatness.

> *You have the power to say yes to the right types of activities and the freedom to say no to other pursuits.*

Let's explore four dimensions that will shape your next steps and guide you toward living out your RIGHT4 YOU Profile: timing, availability, maturity, and development.

TIMING: Evaluate Your Stage and Season of Life

God invites us to be faithful to our callings throughout our lifetime, but different seasons of our lives provide different levels of intensity and availability. God isn't surprised by this, and he knows you need to honor life's seasons.

In one season, you may be getting married. In another you could be starting a family or raising teens. You may be navigating a divorce, working two jobs, finishing college, starting a new job, applying to grad school, caring for littles ones as a stay-at-home parent, grieving a death in the family, adjusting to life as a single parent, or facing a cross-country move. You may be dealing with rotating days off, business travel, a sick child, an elderly parent, seasonal demands, or unemployment.

All these factors need to be considered as you assess when, where, and how to use your gifts to fulfill your God-given passion. The ebb and flow of your involvement requires you to make honest, realistic choices about your schedule so that you honor God—not just with your service, but by living a healthy, balanced life.

Just as you need to eat, rest, and exercise to care for your physical needs, you need to care for yourself spiritually by engaging in spiritual practices that help you connect with God, spend meaningful time with fellow Christ followers who can encourage you and help you grow, and put your spiritual gifts into practice by serving in your area of passion.

You may be at a place in your career where you can contribute additional time and resources to serving, or you may have less to offer. Let God lead. You follow.

A word of caution. Seasons change. Evaluate your current season regularly and make adjustments. Don't let a current *season* of life become a *lifestyle* that keeps you from serving. Even in the busiest of seasons, look for opportunities to use your gifts. We are called to express our gifts, no matter what our season or stage.

> Don't let a current season of life become a lifestyle that keeps you from serving. Even in the busiest of seasons, look for opportunities to use your gifts.

Even if you can't join a team that serves weekly or commit to volunteer regularly, those infrequent opportunities keep you inspired and honor the gifts God has given you. They remind you of the impact you can make and keep you looking forward to the day when a new season will allow you to use your gifts more frequently, permanently, and purposefully.

We're all busy. We're all making choices about how we use our time. When we fail to be regular contributors through using our spiritual gifts in our areas of passion, we can be deceived into thinking we're not really needed. Not true. The fact is, each of us is a part of the body of Christ and has an invaluable contribution to make.

The apostle Paul spells it out beautifully in a letter to the church in Ephesus. "[Christ] makes the whole body fit together perfectly. As each part does its own special work, it helps the other parts grow, so that the whole body is healthy and growing and full of love."[2]

While your contribution may vary with the seasons of your life, it still matters. Listen and be guided by the Holy Spirit for what it means to be a wise steward in every area of your life—your family relationships, marketplace responsibilities, and the all-important contributions you make through your RIGHT4 YOU Profile.

Engage in Sabbath and Sabbaticals

There will be times in your life when you don't just need to redirect your contributions or slow down your involvement, but you need to stop. In Scripture, we read accounts of times and seasons when God's people are told to do nothing—to wait, to be still, to rest. In fact, God set the example himself from the very beginning of recorded history: "[God] rested on the seventh day from all His work which He had done. Then God blessed the seventh day and sanctified it."[3] At designated times, God invites us to rest in his blessing. This principle of the weekly Sabbath was made for us.[4] We are simply to "be" with God, not to "do."

God also instructed his people to steward their property with the principle of Sabbath—to sow and harvest the fields for six years and then on the seventh year to let the land rest. I love the term for this practice: "Year of Jubilee."[5] Who doesn't want a Year of Jubilee?

Taking a sabbatical means disciplining your self to set aside time for rest. There may be seasons in your life when you need to take a serving sabbatical. Without such rest, you're at risk of burnout. Talk to those who know you well. If God is leading you to such a time, it will be confirmed by those around you.

Invest in your sabbatical by attending to your health—physically, emotionally, relationally, and spiritually. Take time for reflection, rest, and renewal.

And don't forget the jubilee! Do things that give you joy and infuse you with energy. Be intentional about slowing down and practicing stillness. Listen for God's quiet voice of guidance as you look to make adjustments in your next season.

AVAILABILITY: Evaluate Your Time

Once you've evaluated your current season of life, it's time to determine your availability. You have twenty-four hours in a day, just like everyone else. No spiritual gifts, relational style, or passion can change that. How many hours do you have available to use your spiritual gifts and pursue your passion?

If you have time to take on something new, it's because you've *made* time to take on something new. You've made choices, and those choices included *not* making time for something else.

When we say we don't have time to do something, many times we're really saying, "I don't want to make the time." Most often, availability is a choice. Saying yes to one opportunity means saying no to other possibilities.

> When we say we don't have time to do something, many times we're really saying, "I don't want to make the time."

Each of us is working with different gifts, styles, passions, maturity levels, and seasons of life, but we all have the same number of hours each day to utilize them. God has given us all the time and resources we need in order to fulfill his calling for our life. The challenge is learning to steward our time so we can accomplish the things we sense God is calling us to do. The apostle Paul put it this way: "Be careful how you live. Don't live like fools, but like those who are wise. Make the most of every opportunity in these evil days. Don't act thoughtlessly, but understand what the Lord wants you to do."[6]

Just as the ways you spend money reveal your financial priorities, your calendar reveals your time priorities. Living your life in response to your RIGHT4 YOU Profile will mean changes to your calendar. It will mean carving out time for new priorities. Making those necessary adjustments to your schedule will flow naturally out of your commitment to God's design and purpose for your life.

How are you organizing your time and energy to express your RIGHT4 YOU Profile? In what ways would you need to increase the time you spend using your spiritual gifts and pursuing your passion? In what areas of your life would you be wise to decrease your time commitments?

When you're stewarding your time, gifts, and passions in a healthy, balanced way, every aspect of your life finds harmony. You have the right amount of time for every one of your God-given priorities—work, relationships, and your contributions to God's kingdom.

> For we are God's handiwork, created in Christ Jesus to do good works, which God prepared in advance for us to do.
>
> *Ephesians 2.10 NIV*

Developing this kind of balanced living takes time. It may not happen this week or this month. It's a journey of making one decision at a time, taking one step at a time toward the fullness of what God has created and called you to. You are on the path toward fulfilling your purpose with your one and only life.

MATURITY: Evaluate Your Spiritual Stage

As you explore different areas where you can use your spiritual gifts, take into account your current level of development as a Christ follower.

Some positions and roles are best filled by people with higher levels of life maturity and ministry experience.

For instance, if you are a new or young Christian with the gift of teaching, it may be challenging for you to lead a Bible study at church or in the marketplace. This doesn't mean you cannot use your teaching gift; rather, it may mean you first need to seek out a mentor who can help you grow in your faith and your understanding of Scripture. More time may be needed for you to grow in your spiritual maturity before you can unleash your God-given gift to its fullest potential.

It's difficult to get where you want to go without being sure of where you are today. By taking an honest spiritual snapshot of yourself today, you will gain more clarity for how you can best move forward with your RIGHT4 YOU Profile. If you were to take a spiritual snapshot of your relationship with Christ today, how would you describe yourself?

Exploring or Unsure

Those who describe themselves as exploring or unsure are in the process of gaining a better understanding of who God is and what it means to be a follower of Christ. They're investigating Christianity and participating in opportunities that enable them to grow in their relationship with God as they walk alongside Christians.

New or Young Believer

Someone who recently became a Christian is often excited and enthusiastic about their new walk with Jesus Christ. Others may have been following Christ for a long time, but they're just now learning what Jesus meant when he promised us his Holy Spirit and an abundant life. Still others are young in age and simply have not logged enough years on planet Earth to grow deeper in their faith. New or young believers are in the process of learning what it means to walk daily in a personal relationship with Christ.

Growing Believer

A growing believer feels confident in God's faithfulness and is pursuing God's direction in their life. They are teachable and sensitive to the Spirit's leading, exhibiting the stability that comes from knowing Christ, regularly worshiping with his people, and actively pursuing a life of greater devotion and service.

Guiding Believer

A guiding believer has reached a level of maturity in their faith where they regularly model Christlike living and inspire others, believers and nonbelievers alike. They lead by example, guiding others into a deeper understanding of what it means to follow Christ and use their spiritual gifts, relational style, and passion out of love to transform lives and communities.

SELF-CHECK: Spiritual Maturity

Think of these four distinctions as a way to capture your spiritual snapshot. It is time-sensitive. It reflects where you are currently. Having read the descriptions above, where would you place yourself spiritually today?

Exploring/Unsure   New/Young   Growing/Stable   Leading/Guiding

As you grow spiritually, your life becomes more attuned to the ways of Christ. You'll more readily reflect love as your primary motivator as you serve others and use your spiritual gifts to honor God.

DEVELOPMENT: Evaluate Your Education, Skills, and Experiences

Just as timing, availability, and maturity guide your next steps, so will your personal development.

To best fulfill your calling, you may need more education, training, or skill development. You may also need more experience alongside a mentor/coach, or as an apprentice or intern. Wherever you are in your development today is fine. But as you look to the future, consider what it will take to grow into what you sense God is calling you to do with your gifts, style, and passion.

You may not be ready or able to take some of these steps now, but you can begin praying to identify what steps you want to take and begin exploring what they might look like moving forward.

Remember, your RIGHT4 YOU Profile indicates how God created you, so by definition you have the power and resources within you to fulfill your calling.

Your journey involves moving from one point to the next. You've been called by God to embark on a journey from today into your future—a journey that is uniquely yours. May each of us "walk in a manner worthy of the calling with which [we] have been called"[7]—and in doing so, may we fulfill our true, God-given purposes.

> *Your destination is a journey, and part of that journey is to develop and mature along the way.*

Your destination is a journey, and part of that journey is to develop and mature along the way.

YOUR DEVELOPING SELF

As you examine your full profile, does the person described on the page sound like the real you? Does it excite you to think of what your life could be like if you lived out each aspect of your profile . . . simultaneously?

Your profile results are like a snapshot of you as a growing and developing person. It captures you at a specific moment in time.

If I were to see a photo of you from ten years ago, I imagine you would look a little different in the photo than you do today. But my guess is that I'd still be able to tell that the person in the picture is you.

The same is true of your RIGHT4 YOU Profile. The inner "selfie" you took of yourself while reading this book and completing these assessments will age with you over time. In a few years, the results of your profile may look a little different. The essence of who God made you to be will remain the same, but your understanding of yourself will become clearer, and thus you'll be better able to reflect your true self to the world.

Your life is a journey in which, as the years go by, you bring your self into better focus. Don't be discouraged if you're not where you wish you were just yet; instead, continue to make necessary changes as you go. Prayerfully discern and give wise attention to your timing, availability, maturity, and development so you can live a life that better aligns with God's purposes for you in each new season.

FOCUSED PRAYER

Lord,
thank you for the changing seasons of my life.
I want to honor you in and through each of them.
Help me steward my time.
Show me how to make the most
of this current stage of my life.
Help me navigate my availability.
Guide me to make wise choices and
prioritize my responsibilities.
Help me grow in maturity.
Teach me more about your Word and your Spirit
so I may become a more fully devoted follower.
Help me maximize my development.
Expand my education and experiences,
so I can grow in grace and in service.
Give me the courage to ask questions,
the willingness to listen,
and the humility to seek mentors and coaches.
Show me my strengths as well as my weaknesses,
and help me turn those weaknesses into strengths.
Give me the power to say yes—and the freedom to say no.
In Jesus' name.
Amen.

REFLECTION:
Questions for Journaling and Discussion

1. Which of the following do you think will be the most difficult for you to navigate moving forward? Explain.
   - Time
   - Availability
   - Maturity
   - Development

2. What are some of your initial thoughts about what you will need to do (or not do) in order to move toward God's purpose for your life?

3. How important do you think rest is in your life's journey? Do you take a regular sabbath? If so, is it weekly? Monthly? How might your life be more fruitful if you incorporated a sabbath into your life's rhythm?

4. Did you find it helpful to think about your spiritual growth in terms of the four stages? Why? Where would you identify yourself today?
   - Exploring or unsure
   - New or young believer
   - Growing believer
   - Guiding believer

5. What do you think Bruce means when he says, "Your destination is a journey"? Do you agree or disagree? Explain.

WHERE IS IT WRITTEN?

Scriptures for Further Study

Then I heard the voice of the Lord, saying, "Whom shall I send, and who will go for Us?" Then I said, "Here am I. Send me!" Isaiah 6.8

1 Samuel 3.4a	Luke 8.11–15
Ecclesiastes 3.1–13	Ephesians 5.15–17
Isaiah 40.31	2 Peter 3.17–18

THE PURPOSEFUL YOU

△13△ THE HEART OF THE MATTER

I was driving across town recently when the brake lights of the cars ahead of me caught my attention. Traffic slowed. Several police cars were stopped on both sides of the road, their lights flashing.

As I drove through this gauntlet of activity, I saw a group of about twenty men picking up roadside trash, all of them wearing bright blue and white jumpsuits. Security guards stood watch on both ends of the group. It appeared that they were doing community service.

The men moved slowly along the side of the road, carrying long sticks and orange trash bags. They would poke a piece of trash with their stick, slowly raise it up, perhaps gaze around for a bit, and then put the trash into the plastic bag. After another step or two, they would poke at something else, slowly pick it up, and put it in the bag.

This group was thorough, but they wouldn't win any speed records for their efforts. It was a nice day, and they were not moving fast or working hard. Their posture and movements lacked focus and enthusiasm, which made sense: they held no particular passion for keeping our highways clean; they were just serving their mandatory time.

I didn't give this experience much thought until a few weeks later. I was driving on a different road when, once again, brake lights lit up in front of me. As I slowed, I passed a group along the roadside, all with matching T-shirts for their church's youth group. They were also doing a community service project to improve their town by picking up roadside trash. The students were running from one spot to the next, poking trash with their sticks and shoving it into their bags. They were laughing and talking, trying to see who could fill their bag first.

What a contrast! The first group had demonstrated apathy and indifference, while the students saw picking up trash as a way to serve God and their community—and they did so with a contagious enthusiasm.

LOVE MAKES A DIFFERENCE

God's love is life-giving. His love motivates us. Let's look at what Scripture says about how God's people are to function together—and what this shows us about love.

The most extensive New Testament passage on the ideal functioning of a community of believers is found in 1 Corinthians 12–13. We've already drawn a great deal of understanding from chapter 12, in which the apostle Paul's analogy of a human body describes how every member of the body of Christ is essential. This passage provides a theological and practical understanding of how the people of God are to function as the body of Christ.

Next comes 1 Corinthians 13, the famous "love" chapter. Despite the fact that this passage is often read at weddings, its focus is not on marriage; the focus is on how we relate to one another and how we use our spiritual gifts. Chapter 12 concludes its teaching on spiritual gifts, and chapter 13 begins with the way spiritual gifts are to be expressed. Notice how God's gifts relate to love:

And yet I will show you the most excellent way.
If I speak in the tongues of men or of angels [gift],
but do not have love, I am only a resounding gong or a clanging cymbal.
If I have the gift of prophecy and can fathom all mysteries and all knowledge, and if I have a faith that can move mountains [gift],
but do not have love, I am nothing.

If I give all I possess to the poor and give over my body to hardship that I may boast [gift],

but do not have love, I gain nothing.

1 Corinthians 12.31–13.3 NIV, emphasis added

God sees love as critical for personal and kingdom success. In his eyes, you can know your spiritual gift and be using it, but if you're not expressing your gift in love, your contribution counts for nothing. It won't last. You won't make the difference he intended for you to make.

To describe this type of love, Paul uses the Greek word *agapē* (ἀγάπη). *Agapē* love is selfless, sacrificial, and unconditional. It puts others ahead of your self. It's the type of love Jesus models, and it is considered to be the highest type of love found in the Bible.

Paul gets specific in describing *agapē* love. Verses 4–8 provide us with a kind of checklist to measure whether our actions and the use of our gifts demonstrate love:

Love is patient, love is kind. It does not envy, it does not boast, it is not proud. It does not dishonor others, it is not self-seeking, it is not easily angered, it keeps no record of wrongs. Love does not delight in evil but rejoices with the truth. It always protects, always trusts, always hopes, always perseveres.

Love never fails.

1 Corinthians 13.4–8 NIV

One easy way to check whether you're expressing this type of love is to reread this passage and insert your own name in place of the word *love*. This little exercise helps you assess the degree to which you are expressing each characteristic. In the self-check below, put your name in the blank and then read each phrase aloud. Seeing, reading, speaking, and hearing each phrase will help you be more accurate and honest in assessing your love quotient.

The Four Loves

Ancient Greece used four different words to define love, each with a distinct meaning.

Agapē: Unconditional love, sacrificial love, a love that puts the best interests of others before self

Philia: Brotherly/sisterly love

Storgē: Parental/family love

Eros: Physical or sexual love

SELF-CHECK: Love Quotient

1. _____ [your name] is patient.

Seldom		Sometimes		Always
1	2	3	4	5

2. _____ is kind.

Seldom		Sometimes		Always
1	2	3	4	5

3. _____ does not envy.

Seldom		Sometimes		Always
1	2	3	4	5

4. _____ does not boast.

Seldom		Sometimes		Always
1	2	3	4	5

5. _____ is not proud.

Seldom		Sometimes		Always
1	2	3	4	5

6. _____ does not dishonor others.

Seldom		Sometimes		Always
1	2	3	4	5

7. _____ is not self-seeking.

Seldom		Sometimes		Always
1	2	3	4	5

8. _____ is not easily angered.

Seldom		Sometimes		Always
1	2	3	4	5

9. _____ keeps no record of wrongs.

Seldom		Sometimes		Always
1	2	3	4	5

10. _____ does not delight in evil but rejoices with the truth.

Seldom		Sometimes		Always
1	2	3	4	5

11. _____ always protects.

Seldom		Sometimes		Always
1	2	3	4	5

12. _____ always trusts.

Seldom		Sometimes		Always
1	2	3	4	5

13. _____ always hopes.

Seldom		Sometimes		Always
1	2	3	4	5

14. _____ always perseveres.

Seldom		Sometimes		Always
1	2	3	4	5

15. _____ never fails.

Seldom		Sometimes		Always
1	2	3	4	5

Overall, how do you think you're doing? Don't be too hard on yourself. None of us model *agapē* love perfectly. The only one who embodies perfect love is Jesus Christ. He gives us his love freely and unconditionally. When we model this type of love as we use our spiritual gifts, not only are we more effective, but the fruit of our efforts benefits others exponentially.

We all need more of God's love flowing through us. The tasks we do in the name of Christ are not as important to God as the heart from which we do them. What we do out of love lasts. In other words, what is done in Christ will last.

Legend of a Young Artist

A story is told of a famous young artist who showed a recent painting to a friend who was himself an accomplished artist. The painting was of the Lord's Supper. After pondering it for what seemed like an eternity, the friend pointed to the central figure and said, "You don't really love him."

Shocked, the artist replied, "But that's the Lord Jesus Christ!"

"I know," the friend said, "and if you loved him more, you would've painted him better."

"If you loved him more, you would have painted him better."

The young painter received a harsh but honest critique from his friend. If someone was looking at how you're painting your life through your gifts, style, and passion, would they conclude that the central figure in your life is Jesus Christ? Actions speak louder than words, and a picture is worth a thousand words. With our actions, fueled by the love of Christ, we paint a picture of the one we follow.

God has given us his very best—his one and only Son, Jesus Christ. He calls us to give him our very best in return, not out of indebtedness, but out of gratitude and love.

Too often, we offer mediocrity in return. We do what we need to do to get by. But is "good enough" good enough for something we give to God? Are we merely giving him our leftover time, leftover finances, and leftover efforts? Or is he the central focus of our life?

Giving to God out of love requires something from every one of us: sacrifice. Giving God our best requires time, thought, and the resources he provides.

The biblical relationship between your spiritual gifts and your love is foundational to your understanding of life and ministry. God's desire for you is not merely that you would express your spiritual gifts, relational style, and passion, but that you would express them in love.

God only asks from you what he has already given to you—his love. As you examine your life and your contributions in this world, consider this: If you loved God more, would you fulfill your life's purpose better?

If you loved God more, would you fulfill your life's purpose better?

The religious leaders in Jesus' time—a group called the Pharisees—paraded around their spirituality for all to see. They boasted holier-than-thou attitudes and flaunted their spiritual practices. They would literally stand out in public where everyone could hear their loud prayers. But people saw through the act. They could not see God through these leaders; they could see only the Pharisees themselves, because they lacked authentic love . . . and it was obvious.

We all have been a little guilty of spiritual acting.

It's easy to scoff at that kind of religious showmanship. But let's be real: we all have been a little guilty of spiritual acting. Recognizing our inner Pharisee is the first step to keeping it real with God and being authentic with others.

So what about you? What is it that motivates you—at home, at work, and in the ways you relate to and serve others? Here's a quick self-check to help you think through your motivation to serve God and others out of love.

SELF-CHECK: Motivation

1. I serve out of love rather than obligation.

Seldom		Sometimes		Always
1	2	3	4	5

2. I care about what God sees rather than what others see.

Seldom		Sometimes		Always
1	2	3	4	5

3. My agenda is God first rather than me first.

Seldom		Sometimes		Always
1	2	3	4	5

4. I demonstrate humility rather than pride.

Seldom		Sometimes		Always
1	2	3	4	5

5. My attitude is "I'll do whatever it takes" rather than "It's not my job."

Seldom		Sometimes		Always
1	2	3	4	5

6. I desire results that are God-honoring rather than self-seeking.

Seldom		Sometimes		Always
1	2	3	4	5

7. I seek to make a lasting impact rather than a good first impression.

Seldom		Sometimes		Always
1	2	3	4	5

Do you see a few areas you'd like to improve? That's normal. On this side of heaven, we all have areas to improve.

Jesus spoke extensively about love. He reminded his followers, "By this all people will know that you are My disciples: if you have love for one another."[1] The development of your character flows out of your relationship with God. The more you develop as a fully devoted follower of Jesus Christ, the greater evidence of love your life will reflect. Love that expresses itself in action is a testimony to the reality and presence of God in your life. It affects the quality of your relationships, the quality of your life, and your ability to fulfill your calling.

FOCUSED PRAYER

Lord,
I've got a lot to learn about love.
I'm more self-centered than I'd like anyone to know,
and I'm often asking the subconscious question,
What's in it for me?
Lord, forgive my selfishness,
and begin a new work of love in my heart.
Teach me to use my spiritual gifts,
personal style,
and life passion
for your glory.
Teach me to love you more
so that I can serve you better.
In Jesus' name.
Amen.

REFLECTION:
Questions for Journaling and Discussion

1. Think of a time when you accomplished something good, but you did it with . . .
    - apathy and indifference: Why do you think you felt apathetic or indifferent?
    - contagious enthusiasm: Why do you think you felt enthusiastic? What does this tell you about how you're wired?
2. At this point in your life, what are your greatest motivations to serve and use your gifts?
3. Which of the qualities from your Love Quotient (pages 150–52) is easiest for you to express? Which is hardest?
4. "If you loved God more, you would serve him better." Do you agree or disagree with this statement? Explain.
5. Describe the difference between someone who is loving but not using their spiritual gifts and someone who is using their spiritual gifts but is not very loving. How do you think each is viewed by others? By themselves? By God?
6. How do you avoid being addicted to mediocrity in your life?
7. What do you most need to do to increase your motivation to fulfill your life purpose?

WHERE IS IT WRITTEN?
Scriptures for Further Study

You were called to freedom, brothers and sisters; only do not turn your freedom into an opportunity for the flesh, but serve one another through love. Galatians 5.13

Matthew 5.16	Acts 2.42–47
John 13.35	1 Corinthians 12–13
John 15.8–11	1 John 4.8

14 WHO HAS YOUR EAR?

My heart sank. I couldn't believe my ears. My doctor was uttering words that would strike fear in anyone: "You have cancer."

I was a husband and father of four little kids, and I had come to the doctor's office to have a lump on my knee examined. Now I'd just been diagnosed with chondrosarcoma—or bone cancer—in my right leg.

For the three days after this grim report, a team of oncologists pored over my medical records as they formed a plan of attack. And for those three days, I waited.

My mind surged with terrible possibilities. Was my disease limb-threatening or life-threatening? Had it spread? Would I be there to walk any of my three young daughters down the aisle at their weddings? Would I be able to play catch with my son? Would my wife be facing the financial and emotional challenge of raising four children alone?

By God's grace, that frightening episode led me to a path of healing and health. Through a somewhat experimental procedure, the cancerous tumor in my knee was removed, preserving both my leg and my life. Since my chondrosarcoma wouldn't respond to chemo or radiation, I underwent surgery to remove the tumor. Doctors felt confident they had gotten all the cancer, but only time would tell.

Dozens of X-rays, CT scans, and examinations took place over the next several years. At my five-year checkup, my heart raced. Five years is a major milestone for cancer sufferers. An "all clear" on that day would mean I was officially considered cancer-free.

The usual X-rays of my leg were taken, and then I waited in an exam room for my doctor to tell me the results. I silently offered thanks for the additional years God had given me and wondered how many more I might have.

My thoughts were interrupted as the doctor, his intern, and a nurse entered the room. The nurse smiled and tried to make conversation. The intern went straight toward a pile of papers on the counter. The doctor pulled up my X-rays on the screen.

The bones and metal brace inside my right leg illuminated before us. With the intern looking over his shoulder, the doctor stared intently, examining one of the X-rays, eyes fixed on the shadowy picture. Deep in thought, he shifted his weight back and forth, restlessly moving one

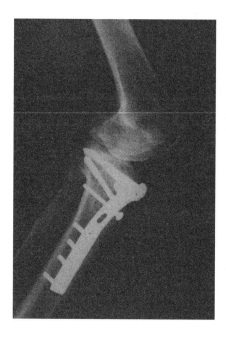

hand in and out of his white coat pocket while unconsciously clicking a pen in the other.

My heart pounded in the silence. *Does he see something?* I waited for him to speak.

Still staring at the X-ray, he spoke. "No evidence of cancer," he pronounced. "You're clear. Congratulations!" Then, before I had time to shout, "Yay, God!" he asked, "Are you ready for knee replacement surgery?"

Huh?

He then pointed at some shaded areas in the X-ray. "Your knee is bone-on-bone. You have no cartilage left as a result of the radical surgery. You must be in a lot of pain," he explained. Turning to face me, he added, "That's an automatic prescription for the inevitable development of arthritis. If you're experiencing too much pain already, I'd recommend going ahead with a knee replacement."

"Thanks, but I'm actually not having any pain or discomfort at all," I said.

"Really?" he asked. "That's great! Well then, no need for surgery. Over the years, I've learned to treat the patient, not the X-ray."

I left his office that day with the cloud of cancer lifted and no plans for knee surgery. I would hold off on the knee replacement until I felt I needed it.

My doctor had listened to me. It must be much easier for doctors to read an X-ray than to read a person. People are emotional. They can be unpredictable. Their feelings are subjective. But my doctor had not trusted his eyes. He trusted me, the patient, who knew my own pain levels despite what the X-ray showed. He took my experience into account before recommending a course of action, which was, in my case, no action.

WHO DO YOU LISTEN TO?

Maybe you're thinking, *Nice story, Bruce, but what does this have to do with me and my life's purpose?* Actually, it has a great deal to do with it. Who you listen to can make a big difference in what you do next.

While it's important to seek input from trusted friends and mentors when it comes to understanding who we are, not every word of advice—even from a wise person—will be wise. Not every word will reflect God's wisdom. Sometimes people just get it wrong, and it takes discernment to know how much sway we should give each person's input.

The apostle Peter is a great example of this in two scenes from the gospel of Matthew.[1] Here's what happened:

Scene one: It was toward the end of Jesus' life and ministry, and people in the community still weren't sure what to make of him. Jesus gathered his twelve closest followers and asked, "Who do people say that the Son of Man is?" His followers gave a little report of all the differing things people had been saying. Some were saying Jesus was just another prophet, others that he was Elijah or John the Baptist reincarnated. It was pretty crazy.

So Jesus asked them directly, "But who do you yourselves say that I am?"

Peter spoke up boldly. "You are the Christ, the Son of the living God!" he said.

Jesus affirmed Peter's declaration, basically replying, "You're right—and it was God himself who revealed this to you." Peter had spoken wisely. These were true words that reflected God's truth.

Scene two (in the very next paragraph): Jesus knew his days on earth were drawing to a close—and that it would not end well for him physically. He began preparing his close followers for what was to come.

Again Peter spoke boldly. He pulled Jesus aside and said, "God forbid it, Lord! This shall never happen to You!"

Good ol' Peter. He meant well. But Jesus knew better. He knew that his death and resurrection were actually part of God's plan.

Jesus turned to Peter and said, "Get away from me, Satan! You are a dangerous trap to me. You are seeing things merely from a human point of view, not from God's."

Ouch!

Peter #1 heard from the Holy Spirit of God and simply spoke what the Spirit said. Peter #2, speaking from a human point of view, missed the mark. What he heard this time were not God's thoughts. Same guy, different words, and hugely different responses from Jesus. Peter #1 got praise and affirmation; Peter #2 got rebuke and correction.

Not every word from someone's mouth reflects God's thoughts. Sometimes their words simply reflect a human point of view. When it comes to discerning your next steps, who you listen to—and how much weight you give their words—matters.

Think of your RIGHT4 YOU Profile as an X-ray of your inner world. With it, you can see more clearly the relationships between your spiritual gifts, relational style, and life passion.

As you begin sharing more of who you are with family, friends, and trusted mentors, some of them may not understand or agree with your commitment to follow Jesus Christ and fulfill God's plan for you. They may offer different ideas as to what you should do with your life. That's normal. Change is hard, not only for you, but also for those who love you. They may prefer that you stay the same.

If people around you resist your newfound clarity about your spiritual gifts, relational style, or passion, it's tempting to second-guess yourself.

Don't do it.

While a spouse, a pastor, a close friend, someone you are dating, a boss, or a leader should have your best interests at heart, sometimes their feedback can run counter to the results of your profile. When this happens, you'll need to decide whose voice you will follow. Just like I needed to push back when my oncologist suggested knee replacement, you may need to push back when well-meaning friends and loved ones offer counsel that doesn't fit. If that's the case, you'll need to set aside their input and continue forward.

But what if several people give you the same (or similar) feedback? What if they stumble upon a theme? Pay attention. Get curious about yourself. We all have blind spots. Have you missed something? Is there an area where you're not seeing yourself clearly or accurately?

Ultimately, you need to make the final decision about what direction your life will take. Only you—not anyone else—will answer to God for how you invest your one and only life, according to your understanding of how God created and called you.

> *Only you—not anyone else—will answer to God for how you invest your one and only life, according to your understanding of how God created and called you.*

So now what? How can you take steps to better align your life to your RIGHT4 YOU Profile and carve out a future of greater faith, fulfillment, and fruitfulness?

ALIGNING YOUR SELF-PERCEPTION

Throughout the book, we've examined how important it is to base our sense of self on who God says we are, not on the opinions of others. We've acknowledged that even from a young age each of us received inappropriate and inaccurate messages about who we are, whether from parents, friends, teachers, pastors, employers, or other people along the way. Just like the grown elephant who believed her stake kept her pinned to the ground, we may have become tethered to these messages. God invites us to break free and embrace our true selves.

This journey toward self-acceptance requires time, reflection, and prayer. Letting go of a false or inaccurate identity can be challenging. If you find yourself stuck, unable to break free from old messages that hinder you from becoming who God created and called you to be, then pray and seek out wise leaders or professional counselors who can help you unpack the origins of those messages and walk alongside you with the Holy Spirit as you release them.

Spend whatever time it takes to settle into your self. Get comfortable with the gifts, style, and passion God has given you and celebrate your *true* self wholeheartedly.

ALIGNING YOUR ROLES

Life is filled with roles we accept for a variety of reasons. Your job requires you to fulfill certain roles that may or may not fit how you prefer to function within an organization. Maybe you said yes to a volunteer position because the need was great, even though you're not passionate about that particular cause. Or maybe you slipped into an unofficial role at church or in a small group, and you wonder if it's an ideal fit for your spiritual gifts.

How do you know if a role is right for you?

A Clarifying Question

A friend once asked me a question that instantly clarified whether or not I should continue doing what I was doing in the way I was doing it. Here's what he said: "Why are you doing what others can do while leaving undone what only you can do?"

Wow! That simple question helped me recalibrate my focus. I immediately recognized that my role on a particular team was actually costing me more than I realized. It was sapping my joy and I wasn't being very fruitful, but I liked the people and they needed my help.

> "Why are you doing what others can do while leaving undone what only you can do?"

My friend's question helped me realize two important lessons: (1) I was keeping someone else from fulfilling a role that fit them, and (2) I was neglecting the primary roles I was more uniquely designed to fulfill. It was a lose-lose situation.

Why was I still in that role? It took me a while to answer the question. Some of my reasons were semi-noble (*I want to be helpful, their mission is important,* and the like), others less so (*The role makes me look good, I'm afraid to disappoint the leader by quitting,* and the like). Bottom line: I needed to step out of that role and make room for something else that fit me better. Which is what I did.

My friend's clarifying question gave me the freedom to unapologetically say no to roles that don't fit who God made me to be and the power to say yes to the right roles as they present themselves in my life.

As you consider current roles in your life, how would you answer that question? What becomes clear to you as a result of your response?

But It's My Job . . .

Sometimes we must fulfill roles simply because they're part of a job that otherwise is a good fit. But if you're regularly finding that your roles, tasks, and responsibilities run counter to who God made you to be, it might be time to consider looking for a position that works *with* your true self rather than *against* it.

Sadly, many busy leaders ask their people to do whatever their organization needs rather than staffing their organization according to each individual's God-given strengths. No job, of course, is free from occasional requirements that don't fit each individual perfectly. It's unrealistic to expect a boss to ask their staff to work only within their ideal sweet spots or to think we can skate through life simply cherry-picking the tasks that suit us best.

If, however, you work or volunteer for someone whose sole focus is getting the job done with little or no concern for your development or job satisfaction, take note. Ask yourself, *Is this worth it? Or should I look for a role that better suits me, with a leader who values the gifts and strengths God has given me?*

It takes time for leaders to truly understand their people and help them identify their gifts, styles, and passions, so it's understandably tempting for leaders to just go for a quick fix instead. This is especially true for churches, nonprofits, and other organizations that rely heavily on volunteers. Their urgency to find someone—anyone with a pulse—may be understandable, but when leaders simply plug holes with people rather than find the right person for each role, it ultimately creates frustration, ineffectiveness, and increased turnover.

While a "just do what I tell you to do" mindset may be necessary in a crunch, it doesn't make sense for the long-term success of any organization. A wise leader invests in people for the long haul. It takes them a little more time on the front end, but it saves countless hours in the long run. The dividends are huge because when the right people are in the right place, the individual, team, customer, and entire organization thrive. Everyone wins!

LEAVING WELL

When people are working side by side in teams, conflict is inevitable. It's human nature. In most cases when conflict occurs, conversations that are honest, respectful, and timely can restore and build healthy relationships.

But what if the conflict won't resolve, despite your best efforts? What if it's causing damage to the team's culture and effectiveness—and your own mental health?

If you're facing relational tension, quitting should be a last resort, not an easy way out. Conflict resolution is to be pursued, not ignored or avoided. Don't let the conflict be an excuse to avoid facing your own contributions to a problem. Instead, first focus on developing your character by owning what you need to own and forgiving the wrongs of others.

If you know a role just isn't right or healthy for you, don't linger. Provide your leaders with adequate time to work out an appropriate transition plan.

Every hour invested in the wrong fit is an hour you're taking from someone else who belongs there—and an hour you're missing out on doing what you do best. Stop doing things that others can do—and start doing what only you can do!

Do it with grace and in love.

If you leave well, there's no need to wallow in guilt or regret. God employs us . . . and in his time, he deploys us. And no doubt the next role you accept will be a better fit for you.

FOCUSED PRAYER

Lord,
thank you that in the midst of all the voices,
I can count on your one true voice.
While there will always be changes in my life,
you are never changing.
Heaven and earth will pass away,
but your words will never pass away. [2]
You are the same yesterday, today, and forever.
Thank you for the way you continually extend your love to me,
and for inviting me into a spiritual journey
that draws me closer to you.
Help me embrace where I am today—
and find next steps that will
help me grow to be more like you
as I am fulfilling my life's purpose.
Amen.

REFLECTION:
Questions for Journaling and Discussion

1. Describe a time in your life when you discovered that what seemed to be true was not really true. What was that experience like? How did you feel?
2. When you get conflicting input or suggestions from others, how do you make your decision? Are you more likely to follow the voices around you or God's voice within you? Why?
3. How would you answer the question, "Why are you doing what others can do while leaving undone what only you can do?"
4. Do you feel you need to make a relational or positional transition? What is moving you to do so? What will be your first step in this transition?
5. If you are in a misfit role or relationship, what part of it do you need to own? What will it look like for you to make it right or "leave well"?

WHERE IS IT WRITTEN?
Scripture for Further Study

"If anyone has ears to hear, let them hear."

Mark 4.23 NIV

Psalm 51.10–12
Matthew 16.13–23

Romans 12.18
1 Corinthians 1.10–13

15 INTENTIONAL LIVING

LIFETIME GUARANTEE

Did you know that God has given you a lifetime guarantee? A guarantee is a promise or assurance, especially in writing, that a specific commitment or benefit will be satisfactorily performed for a given length of time. Every guarantee has a guarantor, the one who assures its fulfillment. And throughout the pages of Scripture, God has given us a number of powerful guarantees. He ensures them. We call them his promises.

GOD'S PROMISES

God not only designed and created you with a purpose; he also made a promise to be with you every step of the way. The apostle Paul articulates this promise: "Being confident of this, that he who began a good work in you will carry it on to completion until the day of Christ Jesus."[1]

God isn't a quitter. If he started something, you can know with certainty that he will complete it. God began a work in you—a good work—and he will finish it, "because God has said, 'Never will I leave you; never will I forsake you.'"[2] That's his promise—and your guarantee!

I love how my friend Loren Van Woudenberg puts it: "God loves you just the way you are. He loves you so much that he doesn't want you to stay the way you are." God's intention for your life was established before the beginning of time: "We are God's handiwork, created in Christ Jesus to do good works, which God prepared in advance for us to do."[3]

Each phrase is packed with meaning.

> **For we are God's handiwork.** The present tense *are* means that God is still at work in our daily lives, developing the tasks we undertake to bring his kingdom to earth. He is alongside us every step of the way.
>
> **. . . created in Christ Jesus.** God's desire is for us to enter into a relationship with him through Jesus Christ. Paul writes, "This means that anyone who belongs to Christ has become a new person. The old life is gone; a new life has begun!"[4]
>
> **. . . to do good works.** God gave each of us a purpose. The tasks to accomplish that purpose are our "good works." We cannot find fulfillment in life apart from participating in the good works he set aside for us to do.
>
> **. . . which God prepared in advance.** God gave thoughtful attention to his plans for us and then paved the way by preparing our work in advance.
>
> **. . . for us to do.** His plans for you are specific and you-shaped. They reflect your role as a meaningful contributor in this world.

As you align yourself with who God made you to be, know this: You are not alone. God is with you every step of the way.

STEPPING OUT OF THE BOAT

Let's look at one more interaction between Jesus and Peter. Peter was a simple, first-century disciple who had a fishing business with his brother. Jesus called them to leave their homes and business to follow him. Peter did not fully grasp his call at the time, but as he continued to follow Jesus, he discovered God's greater purpose for his life. (*And you will too!*)

Here's the first story that stands out to me.[5]

Toward the end of a busy day, Jesus told his followers to go ahead of him and sail across the Sea of Galilee, and he'd meet them on the other side. Many of them were experienced sailors who earned their livelihood in those Galilean waters.

That night, a strong headwind came up, causing huge waves to crash against the boat. Near dawn, Jesus approached them, walking toward their boat across the water! They were terrified. They thought they were seeing a ghost.

Then Jesus spoke. "Take courage! It is I. Don't be afraid."

Still not sure, Peter responded to this supernatural sighting with, "Lord, if it's you, tell me to come to you on the water."

Jesus said, "Come."

Peter stepped out of the boat and started walking on the water toward Jesus. Unbelievable! As long as Peter was looking at Jesus, taking one step at a time, he was doing just fine. But then he took his eyes off Jesus and began to focus on his circumstances—the winds and waves around him, and nothing but water beneath. *People don't walk on water*, he may have been thinking. *Who do I think I am?*

Peter panicked, and filled with fear and doubt, he began to sink. He cried out, "Lord, save me!"

Immediately, Jesus reached out his hand and took hold of him and said, "You of little faith, why did you doubt?"

What an incredible story!

I've often heard sermons about Peter's lack of faith in this scene. But what about the others who never got out of the boat? At least Peter had enough faith to follow Jesus' call. Because he trusted Jesus and followed his call, this simple fisherman walked on water, something none of the other boat sitters did, and something he never could have accomplished without Jesus calling him to "come."

I don't know what God is calling you to do with your one and only life. I don't know how or where he'd like you to invest your spiritual gifts, relational style, and passions. Only God knows, and he is calling you to "come."

Remember this: when Jesus says, "Come," and you follow, amazing things can happen—things that can happen only through the power of God.

> **When Jesus says, "Come," and you follow, amazing things can happen—things that can happen only through the power of God.**

Jesus is calling you. He's inviting you into your own walking-on-water adventure. You have been equipped with spiritual gifts, a relational style, and a God-given passion to do the good works he's prepared in advance for you. There is no better way to live.

It's time to step out of the boat.

FOCUSED PRAYER

Lord,
thank you for preparing good works for me to do,
and for equipping me with the specific spiritual gifts
I need to do them,
for empowering me with my own relational style of doing things,
for igniting a passion in me for causes that matter to you.
Now it's time for action.
With an ear to hear your voice,
help me see my self from your perspective.
Give me the faith to step out of the boat
and follow you.
I long to make the difference you created me for.
Help me live every day with intention
so I can be faithful, fruitful, and fulfilled
as I seek to honor you with my one and only life.
Amen.

REFLECTION:
Questions for Journaling and Discussion

1. Read the two statements below. What do they cause you to feel? Comfort, fear, peace, anxiety, hope, challenge, confusion, or _____?
   - "He who began a good work in you will carry it on to completion."
   - "God loves you just the way you are. He loves you so much that he doesn't want you to stay the way you are."
2. When Jesus called out to Peter in the boat and said, "Come," Peter simply obeyed and followed. Because he obeyed, he got to do something truly miraculous. He walked on water! If you were to "step out of the boat" in faith, trusting Jesus, what miracle would you like to experience in your life?
3. What is the most significant manifestation of God's power you have experienced in your life to date?
4. What has been your greatest failure or sense of personal brokenness? How did God restore you and give you hope?
5. Think of the first time you can remember saying yes to Jesus. (Perhaps now will be that time!) Jesus is once again inviting you to say yes and follow him. How will your yes today be different? Explain.

WHERE IS IT WRITTEN?
Scripture Passages for Further Study

I urge you to live a life worthy of the calling you have received. Be completely humble and gentle; be patient, bearing with one another in love. Make every effort to keep the unity of the Spirit through the bond of peace. Ephesians 4.1–3 NIV

He has made everything beautiful in its time. He has also set eternity in the human heart; yet no one can fathom what God has done from beginning to end. I know that there is nothing better for people than to be happy and to do good while they live. That each of them may eat and drink, and find satisfaction in all their toil—this is the gift of God.

Ecclesiastes 3.11–13 NIV

Just as you received Christ Jesus as Lord, continue to live your lives in him, rooted and built up in him, strengthened in the faith as you were taught, and overflowing with thankfulness.

Colossians 2.6–7 NIV

Matthew 4.18–20   John 21.18–21

Matthew 14.22–33   Other: _____

MY RIGHT4 YOU PROFILE

The following pages include three assessments that make up the foundation of your RIGHT4 YOU Profile:

1. Spiritual Gifts Assessment
2. Relational Style Assessment
3. Life Passion Assessment

You may complete these assessments online at www.brucebugbee. com/profiles or within this book, using a pencil or pen. In either case, you may find it helpful to record your results in the profile below for easy reference.

RIGHT4 YOU ONLINE: *brucebugbee.com/profiles*

The purchase price of this book includes a registration code for completing your assessments online. Record your online username, password, and code here for ease of reference.

My username: _____

My password: _____

My registration code: _____

MY RIGHT4 YOU PROFILE

For easy reference, feel free to note your assessment results here.

Spiritual Gifts

Based on my assessment (completed online or on page 181), my top three **spiritual gifts** are:

1. _____
2. _____
3. _____

Relational Style

Based on my assessment (completed online or on page 193), my **relational style** is best described as:

_____ / _____

(People or Task)   *(Structured or Unstructured)*

Life Passion

Based on my assessment (completed online or on page 199), my **life passions** are:

- _____
- _____
- _____

SPIRITUAL GIFTS ASSESSMENT

This assessment will help you determine your top spiritual gift(s). As you read through each statement, ask yourself, *How true is this of me? What has been my level of experience in this area? To what degree does this statement reflect my natural tendency?* Answer according to who you are today, not who you wish you were or think you should be.

DIRECTIONS

1. Read and respond to each statement below, giving yourself a score of 0 to 3, based on the scale provided below.
2. Place your score in the appropriately numbered box on the Spiritual Gifts Tally Card.
3. Add the numbers in each column and enter the total in the corresponding box below that column.
4. Transfer your top three spiritual gifts to your RIGHT4 YOU Profile on page 180.

Score	Meaning
3	Consistently / Definitely true
2	Most of the time / Usually true
1	Some of the time / Sometimes true
0	Never / Not at all true

SPIRITUAL GIFTS TALLY CARD

A	B	C	D	E	F	G	H	I	J	K	L	M	N	O	P	Q	R	S	T	U	V	W
1	2	3	4	5	6	7	8	9	10	11	12	13	14	15	16	17	18	19				
20	21	22	23	24	25	26	27	28	29	30	31	32	33	34	35	36	37	38				
39	40	41	42	43	44	45	46	47	48	49	50	51	52	53	54	55	56	57				
58	59	60	61	62	63	64	65	66	67	68	69	70	71	72	73	74	75	76				
77	78	79	80	81	82	83	84	85	86	87	88	89	90	91	92	93	94	95				
96	97	98	99	100	101	102	103	104	105	106	107	108	109	110	111	112	113	114				
115	116	117	118	119	120	121	122	123	124	125	126	127	128	129	130	131	132	133	134	135	136	137

Total:

Top Three Gifts:

SPIRITUAL GIFTS STATEMENTS

1. I can coordinate people, tasks, and events to meet a need.
2. I enjoy working creatively with wood, cloth, paints, metal, glass, or other materials.
3. I enjoy developing and using my artistic skills (art, drama, music, photography, and so forth).
4. When I see spiritual complacency, I am willing to challenge it.
5. I don't experience anxiety because I am confident that God not only can handle a situation but will do so.
6. I give freely and joyfully to people in financial need or to important projects that need funding.
7. I enjoy working behind the scenes to support the work of others.
8. I view my home as a safe, caring place for friends and guests.
9. I am honored to pray regularly for someone, a need, or a situation.
10. I like to set goals and can motivate and influence others to achieve a mission that advances God's work on earth.
11. I empathize with hurting people and desire to help them in their healing process.
12. I am drawn to the idea of serving in another country or in an ethnic community that is different from my own.
13. I have delivered a timely, crucial, or influential message to others that I sensed came from God while I was praying.
14. I can communicate God's message of love and salvation with clarity and conviction.
15. I establish trust and confidence through long-term relationships.
16. I communicate messages from God's Word effectively.
17. I can readily distinguish between spiritual truth and error, good and evil.
18. I enjoy research and persistently pursue truth.
19. Others often seek me out for advice about personal and spiritual matters.
20. I am careful, thorough, and skilled at managing details.

21. I am skilled in working with different kinds of tools.
22. I help people better understand themselves, their relationships, and God through my artistic expression.
23. I enjoy reassuring and building up those who are discouraged.
24. I have confidence in God's continuing provision and help, even in difficult times.
25. I give more than a traditional tithe (10 percent) of my income to support God's work.
26. I enjoy doing routine tasks that support a project or meet the needs of my team.
27. I enjoy meeting new people and helping them feel welcomed.
28. I enjoy praying for long periods of time and receive promptings about what God wants me to pray for.
29. It's quite natural for me to lead, and it's more comfortable for me to lead than not to lead.
30. I can patiently provide support and care for those going through painful experiences as they work toward stabilizing their lives.
31. I am energized by taking an active role in starting a new team, project, ministry, or business venture.
32. I have sensed insights from God about someone else's life, and when I share those insights with them, it helped them see God's desire for their future.
33. After I shared my faith with others, they prayed to receive Christ into their lives.
34. I can faithfully walk with others over time to provide them with relational and spiritual insights and support.
35. I can simply and practically explain and clarify the meaning of a Bible passage to those who are confused or don't understand its meaning.
36. I have a "sixth sense" and get insights into a person's character based on first impressions.
37. I receive information I sense is from God that I did not acquire through natural means.

38. I can find simple, practical solutions to a problem in the midst of conflict or confusion.

39. I can clarify goals and develop strategies or plans to accomplish them.

40. I can visualize how something should be constructed before I build it.

41. I like finding new, fresh ways of communicating God's truths.

42. I give hope to others by directing them to the promises of God.

43. I easily trust God for extraordinary needs.

44. I manage my money well so that I can free more of it to give away.

45. I willingly take on a variety of odd jobs at church, at work, or in my community to meet the needs of others.

46. I genuinely believe God sends people my way who are looking for a sense of belonging and connection to others.

47. When I pray for others, I am aware that I am caring for them and helping them.

48. I am chosen as the group's spokesperson when in discussion groups.

49. I am drawn toward people who are sometimes regarded as undeserving or beyond help.

50. I relate to others in culturally sensitive ways.

51. I speak biblical truth in a timely and culturally sensitive way in order to strengthen, encourage, and comfort God's people.

52. I'd rather be around non-Christians than Christians so that I can build relationships with them.

53. I enjoy giving practical support, nurture, and spiritual guidance to a group of people.

54. When I speak or teach, people respond to my presentation with action.

55. I recognize phoniness or deceit in someone before it becomes evident to others.

56. I am not satisfied with superficial understanding or speculation; I seek certainty and truth.

186 \\ What You Do Best

57. I am surprised by how many people are unable to solve problems and seem to lack common sense.
58. I can identify and effectively employ the resources needed to accomplish tasks.
59. I am good at working with my hands, and I enjoy doing so.
60. I seek solitude to reflect, innovate, be inspired, and develop my imagination.
61. I reassure those who need to take courageous action in their faith, family, or life.
62. I am unwavering in my belief that God will work in circumstances where human effort alone cannot guarantee success.
63. I choose to limit my spending so I can give away a higher percentage of my income.
64. I see spiritual significance in doing practical tasks.
65. I rarely meet someone I don't like or wouldn't want to include at work, in a social setting, or at church.
66. I pray with confidence because I know that God responds to prayer.
67. I set goals and direct people to accomplish them effectively.
68. I have deep compassion for hurting people.
69. I view the overall picture of a situation and am not hindered by problems along the way.
70. When I have sensed God revealing insights to me about future events or situations, they turned out just as I thought they would.
71. I boldly speak to others about pursuing a relationship with Christ, and I often see a positive response from those who are listening.
72. When I speak gently to someone who is wandering from their faith or drifting from community, they often return.
73. I get frustrated when I see people's lack of biblical knowledge.
74. When someone is causing dissension or speaking against God's truth, I feel God helps me see whether they're speaking from an error in truth, a mental or emotional challenge, or an evil influence.

75. When reading or studying Scripture, I can identify important biblical truths and themes that could benefit others.

76. Looking at the actions of an individual or group, I can anticipate the likely consequences.

77. I like to help groups and teams function with greater efficiency.

78. I work behind the scenes to make things that honor God and can be helpful or useful for others.

79. The way I say and do things seems to spark insight in others, who often tell me, "I've never thought of it that way."

80. I find great joy in affirming the value and worth of others.

81. When I see God's presence and activity, I move toward it despite any opposition or a lack of support.

82. For fundraising campaigns and special projects, I like to contribute financially in a way that inspires others to give generously.

83. I like to find things that need to be done—and do them without being asked.

84. For me, the greatest times of joy are times of social interaction and relational connection.

85. When I hear about a troubling situation, I feel compelled to pray.

86. I motivate others to perform to the best of their ability.

87. I look beyond a person's limitations, problems, or challenges to see a life that matters to God and an opportunity to help them overcome.

88. I value cultural sensitivity and am comfortable with people from different racial, ethnic, gender, and socioeconomic groups.

89. I feel compelled to speak the words I sense God gives me to strengthen, encourage, and comfort others.

90. I talk openly about spiritual things, hoping people will ask me about my faith.

91. I invest in other people, guiding them with truth, encouragement, care, and wisdom.

92. I communicate biblical truths in ways that motivate others to want to know more.

93. Others affirm the reliability of the insights and perceptions I've had about them and others.
94. I have known things about others but did not know how I knew them.
95. I give practical advice to help others through complicated situations.
96. I can visualize a coming event, anticipate potential problems, and develop strategies to overcome them.
97. I am a resourceful person who can find the best materials and tools needed to build whatever is needed.
98. I use various forms of the arts to draw people closer to God and his truth.
99. I like motivating others to take steps toward spiritual growth.
100. I regularly challenge others to trust God.
101. I manage my money and donate to well-led organizations and projects that are making a difference for Christ in the lives of people.
102. I show my love for others in actions more than words.
103. I do whatever I can to make visitors and marginalized people feel like they belong.
104. God gives me a sense of peace that my prayers are being answered, even when I cannot see the results.
105. When I cast a vision for a project or goal, others want to follow and be a part of it.
106. I enjoy bringing hope, joy, and comfort to people who are working through a crisis or chronic difficulty in their lives.
107. I relate to leaders who often follow me into new ventures.
108. I sense God reveals to me certain things others cannot yet see, so that when I speak to them about those things, they can understand God's activity in their lives.
109. I love to connect with people outside of my faith community, no matter where they are in their spiritual journey.
110. I take responsibility for nurturing the whole person in their walk with God.

111. I present information and insights to others in ways that make it easier for them to understand and apply to their lives.

112. I sometimes sense that I can see into the spiritual realm, where spirits have been revealed and identified to me by God.

113. The truths I learn and the understandings I gain create a burden for me because I feel responsible to handle the information wisely.

114. When faced with how to apply biblical truths practically in a difficult or complex situation, I sense God guiding me to a workable solution.

115. I long to bring order to organizational chaos.

116. I have good hand-eye coordination and dexterity.

117. I have a sense of the whole and can communicate a biblical truth artistically by putting things together in a harmonious flow.

118. I carefully challenge or rebuke others in order to help them grow spiritually.

119. I find it natural to believe in God for things that others see as impossible.

120. I have been given an abundance of financial and material resources so I can give more to God's work.

121. When a task needs to be done, I find it difficult to say no.

122. I can make people feel at ease even in unfamiliar surroundings.

123. I see specific results in direct response to my prayers.

124. I figure out where we need to go and help others get there.

125. I am motivated by compassion to remove the source of someone else's sufferings.

126. God's authority and power can be seen in me through the ventures and new places he has led me to.

127. I feel compelled to expose wrongdoing whenever I see it. I am comfortable challenging people to discontinue that behavior and make things right.

128. I'm constantly thinking of ways to bring up spiritual matters with friends who do not know God.

129. I feel responsible to help oversee and protect people from things that might keep them from a relationship with God and each other.
130. When I have been studying, I struggle with communicating only those things that will help God's people learn what they need at the moment.
131. I can sense when evil forces are at work in a person or situation.
132. I love to learn new things and then share them with others.
133. I like to read and study the book of Proverbs because its simple and powerful truths are expressed in such clear and practical ways.

For these final four statements, place a check mark on your tally card if you have *repeatedly* experienced any of the following:

134. I laid my hands on someone and prayed for their healing—and they were physically, emotionally, or spiritually healed and set free.
135. When I hear someone speak in tongues, I sometimes sense God's Spirit revealing that person's message to me, and I can interpret it for the group.
136. I have experienced God's power within me to drive out demons, and the impossible has become possible. I also have witnessed his supernatural intervention in nature.
137. I often speak in a language I don't understand—and someone nearby can interpret what I said.

SPIRITUAL GIFTS KEY

A	Administration	**M**	Prophecy
B	Craftsmanship	**N**	Evangelism
C	Creative Communication	**O**	Shepherding
D	Encouragement	**P**	Teaching
E	Faith	**Q**	Discernment
F	Giving	**R**	Knowledge
G	Helps	**S**	Wisdom
H	Hospitality	**T**	Healing
I	Intercession	**U**	Interpretation
J	Leadership	**V**	Miracles
K	Mercy	**W**	Tongues
L	Apostleship	**Other**	

SPIRITUAL GIFTS SUMMARY

My top three spiritual gifts are:

1. _____
2. _____
3. _____

Transfer these results to your RIGHT4 YOU Profile on page 180.

RELATIONAL STYLE ASSESSMENT

This assessment helps you determine your relational style. As you read the statements on each continuum, ask yourself, *Which preference best describes me?*

Remember, there are no right or wrong responses. Resist the urge to answer according to what a spouse, family member, church leader, or employer expects of you. Select the behavior or perspective that comes most naturally to you when there are no restrictions, pressures, or consequences for your personal self-expression.

DIRECTIONS

1. In the Energized (E) and Organized (O) Scales below, read each preference statement and choose the number along the continuum that best describes you.
2. Total your "E" and "O" scores and write them in the box below each section; then plot your results on the graph provided.

ENERGIZED (E) SCALE

How are you energized? Circle the number that best indicates your preferences on each continuum.

1. I am more comfortable . . .

Doing things for people   1   2   3   4   5   Being with people

2. When doing a task, I tend to . . .

Focus on the goal   1   2   3   4   5   Focus on relationships

3. I get more excited about . . .

Advancing a cause   1   2   3   4   5   Creating community

4. I feel a sense of accomplishment or fulfillment when I . . .

Complete a job   1   2   3   4   5   Build a relationship

5. It is more important to start a meeting . . .

On time   1   2   3   4   5   Once everyone has arrived

6. I am more concerned with . . .

Meeting a deadline   1   2   3   4   5   Maintaining the team

7. I place a higher value on . . .

Action   1   2   3   4   5   Communication

My Energized (E) Scale Total: _____

ORGANIZED (O) SCALE

How are you organized? Mark the number that best indicates your preferences on each continuum.

1. I prefer to ...

Be spontaneous 1 2 3 4 5 Follow a plan

2. I prefer guidelines that are ...

General 1 2 3 4 5 Specific

3. I like to ...

Leave my options open 1 2 3 4 5 Settle things now

4. I prefer projects that have ...

Variety 1 2 3 4 5 A routine

5. I like to ...

Play it by ear 1 2 3 4 5 Stick to a schedule

6. I find routine ...

Boring 1 2 3 4 5 Restful

7. I like to accomplish tasks by ...

Working it out as I go 1 2 3 4 5 Following directions

My Organization (O) Scale Total: _____

GRAPHING YOUR RELATIONAL STYLE

1. **Mark your Energized "E" Scale score on the vertical column** to the left of the graph below. This reflects whether you are more energized by people or tasks.
2. **Mark your Organized "O" Scale score on the horizontal row** below the graph. This reflects whether you prefer to function in a structured or unstructured environment.
3. **Draw a line from left to right** through the mark you placed for your E Scale.
4. **Draw a line from top to bottom** through the mark you placed for your O Scale (see examples below).
5. **Notice in which quadrant your two lines intersect.** Your Personal Style is indicated by that quadrant.

In the example below, the E and O Score lines connect in the "People/Structured" quadrant of our graph.

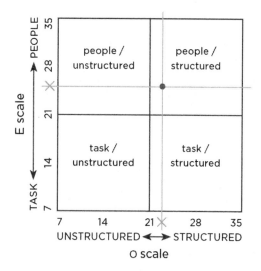

In which quadrant does your intersection fall? Mark your E and O Scale numbers on the graph below and then draw your horizontal and vertical lines to discover your relational style.

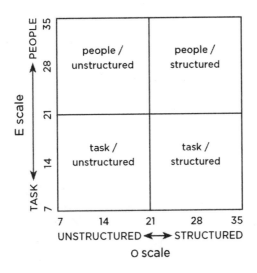

RELATIONAL STYLE SUMMARY

My relational style is best described as:

_____ / _____

(Task or People)   *(Unstructured or Structured)*

Transfer these results to your RIGHT4 YOU Profile on page 180.

LIFE PASSION ASSESSMENT

This assessment helps you identify different ways your God-given life passion may have already shown up in your life. By getting clear on your passion, you'll be better equipped to express that passion (or those passions) through your life, work, ministry, and community activities.

The assessment includes three exercises:

1. Self-Reflection Prompts
2. Positive Experiences
3. Passion Categories

Things to Remember

There are no right or wrong answers. Give yourself permission to write whatever you want. If you don't have an answer for every question or you can't complete every section, that's okay. Just prayerfully consider your responses and do your best to answer honestly.

This is an individual exercise. Complete the assessment on your own, without the influence of others. You can talk about your results with other people afterward if you desire their input.

Dream big. Assume there are no obstacles to hinder you from fulfilling your heart's desire (your life passion). Don't answer a question based on whether you think you could succeed or how you might do so. Assume everything is taken care of—family, money, career, time, and so forth—and simply focus on naming that area of passion.

EXERCISE 1: Self-Reflection Prompts

Prayerfully ponder and respond to the prompts below. Write from your heart to best capture your thoughts, reflections, and emotions.

1. If I could snap my fingers to be guaranteed success, what would I do for others?
2. What regularly annoys or angers me about this world that if changed would honor God or bring the compassion of Christ to others?
3. At the end of my life, I hope to look back and know I've done something to make a positive difference about . . .
4. I care about certain things more than others. I care most about . . .

EXERCISE 2: Positive Experiences

Complete the chart below to capture positive experiences in your life and spot themes or patterns that might give you insight into your life passion. Your experiences may have occurred at home, work, school, or during free time. *Examples: A time you fixed a clock, developed a computer program, comforted a friend, organized an event, had a meaningful conversation, were part of a group, took a trip, received an award, helped someone move, built a house, won an election, or gave to someone in need.*

Directions

1. **List your most meaningful positive life experiences.** Name five to seven experiences that left a positive impact on your life—things you feel good about, even if others didn't notice.
2. **Briefly describe why each experience meant so much to you.**
3. **Look over what you've written.** What theme(s) do you notice? What patterns repeat themselves? Write those themes and patterns below the chart.

	Positive Experience	Why was this experience meaningful to me?	Possible Theme
A			
B			
C			
D			
E			
F			
G			

Recurring Themes

Strongest Recurring Theme: _____

Second-Strongest Recurring Theme: _____

EXERCISE 3: Passion Categories

Some passions center around a people group or a social issue. Consider the lists below and check any that resonate with you. Feel free to add your own group or issue. (Note: It's okay if nothing resonates with you. Perhaps your life passion isn't related to people groups or social issues.)

People Groups

- ☐ Infants
- ☐ Children
- ☐ Teens
- ☐ Teen moms
- ☐ Single parents
- ☐ College students
- ☐ Single adults

- ☐ Divorced people
- ☐ People who are grieving
- ☐ Women in business
- ☐ Young married couples
- ☐ Refugees
- ☐ Parents
- ☐ Empty nesters

- ☐ Ethnic group: _____
- ☐ Racial group: _____
- ☐ Religious group: _____
- ☐ People who are homeless
- ☐ Job seekers
- ☐ Senior citizens
- ☐ People with disabilities

- ☐ Incarcerated individuals
- ☐ People who are poor
- ☐ Hospitalized or sick people
- ☐ LGTBQ+ individuals
- ☐ Homebound people
- ☐ _____

Social Issues

- ☐ Environment
- ☐ Global warming
- ☐ Childcare
- ☐ Gender identity
- ☐ Discipleship
- ☐ AIDS/HIV prevention
- ☐ Politics
- ☐ Violence
- ☐ Gangs
- ☐ Injustice
- ☐ Racism
- ☐ Equal opportunity employment
- ☐ Women's issues
- ☐ Clean water
- ☐ Education
- ☐ Recovery from addiction

- ☐ Mental illness
- ☐ Economics
- ☐ Spreading my faith
- ☐ Technology
- ☐ Health care
- ☐ Poverty
- ☐ Abortion/unplanned pregnancy
- ☐ Hunger/food security
- ☐ Literacy
- ☐ Nutrition and health
- ☐ Equal rights
- ☐ Diversity
- ☐ Censorship
- ☐ Immigration
- ☐ _____

Based on your responses above, which one or two passion categories below best reflect the overall area of your passion?

✓	Passion Category	Description
	Celebration	People with this passion primarily connect with God by engaging in worship, the arts, creativity, the exploration of Scripture, and the like.
	Outreach	People with this passion primarily focus on connecting with others who don't identify as Christians, hoping to lead them into a relationship with Christ and his church and a discovery of his purposes.
	Connection	People with this passion are drawn toward individuals who are unconnected, inviting them into community with Christ and his people through hospitality, encouragement, and a sense of belonging.
	Equipping	People with this passion are generally maturing believers in the development of their spiritual gifts, ministry expertise, and leadership. They seek to develop others through a variety of life stages and affinity-based groups for growth, accountability, and purpose.
	Caregiving	People with this passion enjoy assisting others with their physical, emotional, relational, and spiritual health through the love and resources of God's people.
	Supporting	People with this passion enjoy assisting others from behind the front lines of ministry or marketplace endeavors. They are energized by doing supportive tasks that free others to maximize their kingdom impact.

Understanding the category or categories you're drawn toward might confirm a certain passion area that is becoming clearer to you—or it might not. If you're feeling clear on your life passion but it doesn't easily fit into one of these categories, no problem. The categories are simply another angle to help you narrow down where your passion(s) may lie.

Life Passion Summary

Based on these three exercises, here's how I understand my life passion(s) today:

My life passion is for (or to):

_____

_____

_____

My life passion most closely fits closest this passion category:

_____

_____

_____

Transfer these results to your RIGHT4 YOU Profile on page 180.

ACKNOWLEDGMENTS

Don Cousins is a friend, mentor, coach, and wise leader. We have coauthored books, served together, and continue to seek out God's best for each other. His passion and gifts have served me well because he has been so committed to doing what he does best. Thank you for your faithfulness, Don.

I want to express my deep appreciation for the gifts, passions, and spirit of September Vaudrey, who worked diligently to collaborate and edit this book with me. Her personal and professional perspectives have brought greater clarity and effectiveness to the message.

I also am grateful to the Zondervan Reflective team, who has been supportive to the calling to which I have been called. Thank you, Ryan Pazdur, Alexis De Weese, Dirk Buursma, and Stan Gundry.

My late brother, Larry Bugbee, took the RIGHT4 YOU Profile and spent countless hours preparing to put it online and to make it available in English, Spanish, and Latvian. Thousands around the world will be served and blessed by his contribution. He was loved and is missed.

I appreciate the millennials, boomers, Gen Xers, and Gen Zers for your thoughtful input. We are all a part of "this generation" in God's kingdom as we journey together to fulfill our calling.

I am most grateful to the Head of the church, Jesus Christ. It is because of him that this book has come to be.

NOTES

A Note from the Author

1. John 8.36.
2. Galatians 5.1.
3. Mother Teresa, *The Joy in Loving: A Guide to Daily Living* (New York: Penguin, 1996), 276.

Chapter 1: Intentional Creation

1. See Philippians 4.11.
2. Mark 12.31.
3. See John 13.1–17.
4. Matthew 6.10.

Chapter 2: Who Does God Say You Are?

1. See Isaiah 64.8; Jeremiah 18.1–6; see also Romans 9.20–21.
2. See Matthew 4.18–19.
3. See Acts 9.1–31.
4. See 1 Samuel 1.1–2.11.
5. See 1 Samuel 16.6–23; 2 Samuel 2.
6. See Judges 4.4–10.
7. See Judges 6.1–7.22.
8. See Exodus 2–18.
9. See Matthew 1.18–2.11.
10. See John 1:1–27.
11. 1 Samuel 16.7 NIV.
12. Ephesians 2.10 NIV.

Chapter 3: What's the Big Deal about Spiritual Gifts?

1. 1 Corinthians 12.1.
2. See 1 Corinthians 12.14–26.

3. Paraphrased from Jesus' parable of the ten talents, found in Matthew 25.14–30.

Chapter 4: The Benefits of Spiritual Gifts

1. John 15.8.
2. John 15.11.
3. 1 Corinthians 12.27 NIV.
4. Matthew 5.14, 16 NIV.

Chapter 5: You've Got Gifts!

1. This story was adapted from a fable written by George Reavis, assistant superintendent of Cincinnati Public Schools in the 1940s. This content is now in the public domain and is free to copy, duplicate, and distribute.
2. See 2 Corinthians 5.17.
3. Note: If you've lost your code or you're borrowing this book and its code has already been redeemed, you may purchase another unique code from the home page at www.brucebugbee.com.
4. If you don't have access to a printer, write down your results in your journal or on a blank sheet of paper, as well as on page 180 in the spaces provided.

Chapter 6: What Spiritual Gifts Are *Not*

1. Read Jesus' words about being "born again" in John 3.
2. Galatians 5.22–23.
3. Romans 11.29 NIV.
4. 1 Corinthians 13.2.
5. James 2.26.
6. 1 Timothy 4.7.

Chapter 8: Developing Your Style

1. The Gospels are the first four books of the New Testament of the Bible—Matthew, Mark, Luke, and John—each telling the story of Jesus' ministry on earth from their differing perspectives, with their various styles, and for their unique audiences.

Chapter 9: What's the Big Deal about Passion?

1. John 15.7 NIV.
2. See Galatians 1.15–16.
3. See Acts 9.1–31.
4. Romans 11.29 NIV.

Chapter 10: You've Got Passion!

1. If you don't have access to a printer, write down your results on page 180 in the spaces provided.

Chapter 12: Timing, Availability, Maturity, Development

1. Jim Collins, *Good to Great: Why Some Companies Make the Leap . . . and Others Don't* (New York: HarperCollins, 2001), 1.
2. Ephesians 4.16 NLT.
3. Genesis 2.2–3.
4. See Mark 2.27.
5. See Leviticus 25.8–55.
6. Ephesians 5.15–17 NLT.
7. Ephesians 4.1.

Chapter 13: The Heart of the Matter

1. John 13.35.

Chapter 14: Who Has Your Ear?

1. Matthew 16.13–23; all quotes are from the NASB, except for Jesus' final quote (v. 23 NLT).
2. See Matthew 24.35 NIV.

Chapter 15: Intentional Living

1. Philippians 1.6 NIV.
2. Hebrews 13.5 NIV.
3. Ephesians 2.10 NIV.
4. 2 Corinthians 5.17 NLT.
5. See Matthew 14.22–33 NIV.

 **NETWORK MINISTRIES INTERNATIONAL**

Bruce Bugbee & Associates

We want to hear from you! Share what God is unleashing in you and through you as you are discovering and doing what you do best. What is your story?

brucebugbee.com/share

Get more copies of *What You Do Best* for a friend, spouse, classmate, small group, new member class, missions team, or marketplace study.

The book and RIGHT4 YOU Profile are also available in Spanish! Get *Qué es lo que hace major.*

Gather a group and create community around an online video-enhanced experience of *What You Do Best.*

For these and other resources, coaching, and the RIGHT4 YOU Profiles online, go to:

www.brucebugbee.com

Other Books by Bruce Bugbee

Network (Bruce Bugbee, Don Cousins)
  Getting the right people in the right places for the right reasons at the right time

Discover Your Spiritual Gifts the Network Way (Bruce Bugbee)
  Four spiritual gifts assessments plus a ministry assessment tool

Experiencing LeaderShift Together (Don Cousins, Bruce Bugbee)
  A step-by-step strategy for small groups and ministry teams

Experiencing LeaderShift Application Guide (Bruce Bugbee, Don Cousins)
  Transforming program planners and event coordinators into equipping leaders and effective ministry teams